TURNING YOUR LIFE AROUND

The Meditative Beauty of Woodturning

Ron Murray

MUREX PRESS

TURNING YOUR LIFE AROUND : THE MEDITATIVE BEAUTY OF WOODTURNING

Copyright © 2020 by Ron Murray

For information contact : Ron Murray, 1/34 Findlay Street, Ellerslie, Auckland 1051, New Zealand http://www.wrytings.com

Turning Your Life Around – The Meditative Beauty of Woodturning looks at the relatively little-known world of woodturning and how it (like many crafts) provides a healthy escape from the stressful world we live in, particularly as we enter our later years.

Key words : woodturning, meditation, wellbeing, wood, woodworking, contentment, happiness, fulfilment...

A few words on the illustrations

*Photographs in this book are largely by **Callum Post** – a very talented young lensman and videographer - and the author; other sources are as credited. Budget restrictions for my modest publishing venture meant I couldn't afford to run colour photos inside the text, but if you'd like to see the colour versions of the pix in this book – and other wood and turning or turned item images - go to my website www.wrytings.co.nz and check out the section on this book.*

*Cover design by **Jonathan Templeman**, Design Dairy*

Author's note : The small buddha with lit candle and wood-shavings scattered around featured on the cover was for purely figurative and illustrative purposes only ; there is no place for a naked flame in your turning studio. Health & Safety rules, OK ?!

ISBN: 978-0-473-52241-4

First Edition: June 2020

DEDICATION

To those who plant trees.
Without you, in time, our lathes would be idle...

for more than one reason.

CONTENTS

INTRODUCTION

Why. This. Book.

Woodturning is one of those crafts that you either know almost nothing about – or a lot. As a hobby, it may have drifted into your realm of consciousness when you saw a wooden bowl in a souvenir shop– but more likely, it never has.

It's old-fashioned in the sense that carving is. Making bowls and long items like chair legs from wood by rotating the rough wood against a chisel has been a practice since before electricity made the modern lathe possible. Those early practitioners were called "bodgers" and their lathe used a foot-pedal action turning the wood at speed.

Pictured: a modern day bodger's lathe built by Auckland blacksmith Sol Marshall. (Picture: Tim Marshall).

Wooden bowls and platters still abound and people love their "natural" look and simple utility. But glass and pottery jostle for the same space in the cupboard. And not a lot is generally known about how a wooden bowl actually gets made.

Woodturning isn't a "black art" though; there are plenty of books, classes, businesses, and practitioners imparting the techniques and marketing the equipment to turn wood.

Twenty or so years ago I pretty much knew nothing about turning. It didn't even remotely enter my zone of interest. But I did like driftwood. Then one memorable day I was beachcombing at my hometown Mount Maunganui soon after there had been a massive influx of driftwood onto the Bay of Plenty beaches. Tonnes of the stuff – big logs, small chunks and every size in between, output of some huge storm across the East Cape or Coromandel which downed trees, sent them into rivers – and thence to the sea.

Exploring the vast streams of wood, I noticed an older guy picking up some chunky bits and, in casually chatting with him, learnt he was going

A massive log at Papamoa – what fine wood hides inside?

to "turn" some of them. I had to ask what he meant.

Intrigued and curious, I took up his invitation to check out his turning set-up. He lived just over the road from where we were staying and in his small, neatly ordered tin shed he had a lathe, turning tools and finishes – and a collection of turned, lidded vases called – don't ask me why – "boxes" by turners.

I was more than captivated. Hooked. And my turning journey began. Two decades or so on, I have a great lathe and most of the customary turning paraphernalia in a space at the back of my garage. And there is just about always something on the lathe.

But I'm not a professional turner, though I did sell my bowls and platters through a South Island tourist outlet at one stage. Technically, I guess I do an OK job but some of the advanced techniques remain beyond my capability.

So why write a book on it?

There is no real point in producing yet another pure guide to wood-turning – a how-to-do-it book – because there are many excellent ones around that detail the technical processes involved in turning, and finishing your turned items. In teaching myself, I drew on several of them and they're acknowledged in the bibliography at the end of the book.

I wanted to give my account of how to turn, however, since it's an important part of the story. But this book is more about the spiritual value and joy that turning brings. I hear a few groans at the use of the word "spiritual". But – fear not – this is no religious text. I'm an agnostic. I do, however, believe in the importance of having a guiding set of principles and practices that help bring you peace-of-mind and ultimately happiness. Foremost among those is meditation and its sidekick, mindfulness.

Turning, for me, is meditative. And I don't think there'd be a turner on the planet who wouldn't agree that turning is a precious and absorbing activity that hooks you in and never lets you go. Turners' sheds are havens from an increasingly complex and distressing world, places where they can push the world's crap from their minds and transform rough, dull bits of wood into things of beauty.

The meditative side to turning is the essential subject of this book.

People who already turn will (I hope) get my drift and find lots to nod about in the story that follows. But they're already savvy.

Some (maybe many) may think I'm off my rocker – what, *meditation*? My thesis is not at all why *they* turn. For me, it's a bit of a solitary hobby and spare-time occupation. But many people turn for the social side: the club environment, the camaraderie, club evenings, competitions, awards, the buy-and-sell environment, the advice on hand or others keen to hear your advice, the friendships made that endure for life. All gold.

This book is more for people who are perhaps looking for a hobby that will support them on the journey to peace-of-mind and, ultimately, enduring mental health through the challenges of old age and retirement. And that includes early retirement – as I edit this book in early 2020 the world has been rocked on its axis big-time by a virus too

small to see with the naked eye – COVID-19. The disruption and dislocation to our lives is astonishing and well-familiar to readers; having a hobby in the garage through the enforced lockdown here in New Zealand has been a godsend.

Turning is a hobby that combines meditation with the pleasure of creation using one of the earth's most beautiful raw materials. Where you set your goals, and the clock, entirely as you wish.

It's not an instant entry to bliss. Learning to turn is a journey of learning and preparing, then just giving it a go. There will be a few bumps and potholes along the way as you master the techniques and encounter the pitfalls – items that break, wood that turns out rotten. But it could "turn your life around" in an utterly positive way, as my title suggests.

Believe me, when you learn the craft and reach that moment where you are applying the first coat of oil or wax to your turned, sanded bowl or whatever, there is a moment of pure beauty and pleasure that is priceless: like a veil lifted on a beautiful bride, the wood comes to life.

I am reminded of lines from one of my favourite poems, James Wright's "The Blessing":

"Suddenly I realize
that if I stepped out of my body, I would break
into blossom."

This book is my celebration of the pleasure and meditative healing capability I believe turning (and working with wood) brings.

Welcome to the journey.

CHAPTER ONE: THE WONDER OF WOOD

I think that I shall never see / a poem lovely as a tree.
Joyce Kilmer – American poet

Kind of a twee quote to kick off this chapter, but a tree *is* a pretty impressive piece of work. From gnarled little bonsais to huge redwoods, trees are an astonishing part of the botanical spectrum.

They present an immense range of colours and patterns of root, trunk, branch and leaf. In shape and structure they're uplifting and talismanic.

And strong! You see tall ones in pretty hefty winds and they hold their ground – literally.

But they do drop in the worst of storms, sometimes to tragic and devastating effect.

We grow trees for a host of reasons – shelter, crops and, of course, for the timber they provide to build with, or burn as fuel. Timber is used for many items from small *netsuke* carvings to vast houses. It is an incredibly versatile material.

We've all seen homes where natural timber is painted over – which feels like sacrilege. But most users of wood aim to retain the *look* of the raw product. Or better still use it to its best advantage. There are around 60,000 (known) species of timber-producing tree in the world (and no doubt others yet to be discovered hidden away in some unexplored rain forest in South America – before loggers eradicate it).

The look of wood is about colour, depth and grain – and a few other aspects. Many timbers to be fair are quite bland, with perhaps little variation in colour, no depth and no distinction to the grain.

But, thankfully, many many timbers are much livelier. Trees often have a clear distinction between the heartwood at the centre of the trunk and the sapwood – the layer closest to the external bark through which nutrients flow from roots to branches and leaves. There can often be a quite striking difference in colour between heart- and sapwood – as seen in puriri in New Zealand. And the colour range just about works the whole palate from white and cream through fawn, amber and yellow, to brown, chocolate, red, pink, and purple, and even greens and black. Often, it's a swirl of many of those. Enchanting.

Depth (*see photo*) is a wood trick that never ceases to impress. It's a 3-

D illusion that seems to suggest the wood is ridged or furrowed when it's actually flat and smooth. It's often called "figure" and arises from the natural growth process of the wood that a scientist could probably explain but not me.

Depth and figure often are seen to best effect in the bits of a tree that the house-builders discard – the stumps where trunk meets lateral roots and the boles where the trunk flows into outward-projecting branches. Builders want the straight fibres in the trunk timber. The rest is angular, warped, knobbly, knotty and can be annoying to the weatherboard brigade. To the turner it's much more fun, with the promise of interesting figure, but also irregularity of grain.

Grain is the wood's individual signature. It's the pattern – usually reasonably regular – of different coloured lines, swirls, curves, streaks, flecks, spots, patches and so on, strewn through the normal run of the wood's colour.

There are other aspects that add to the look too. One is "spalting", which refers to a natural process of decay in the timber as it lies on the forest floor perhaps. For reasons our scientist again can best explain, certain parts of the wood darken through the rotting process while others stay the same. It's 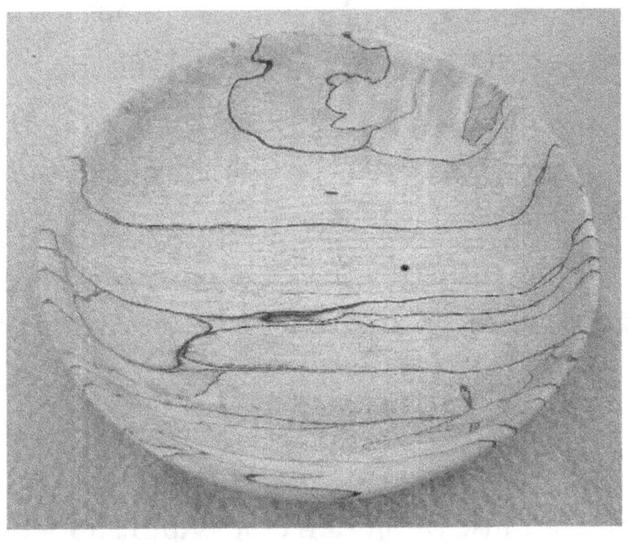 seemingly random and can be spectacularly eye-catching. Tawa in New Zealand is commonly where you sight this sort of effect – intricate black lines on the creamy fawn timber (*pictured*). Left to rot too long, the wood can go spongey in patches though, which ruins its turnability. But there's a sweet spot where the colours have changed and it's still workable and the end results can be pretty cool.

Then there's the whole school of added effects through oils, stains, waxes, acids, fire-torching, and other embellishments.

But to me the best wood speaks for itself.

As noted in the introduction, finishing does amplify the beauty in wood – a little like the difference between opening your eyes underwater unprotected and viewing the same scene through a face-mask.

When you turn wood, it's also like peeling layers off an onion, many many layers, as you work towards the planned shape (though you may still be deciding that as you go – half the fun!) Wood works like a magician that way: it shows you designs and colours but as you turn away layers they may disappear – or something startling may appear from nowhere. Clay and metal, even glass, can't pull that trick.

Some woods are a pure, simple joy to turn. As turners say, they turn like butter. In New Zealand, kauri is like that (almost always), which makes it commercially a smart wood to process (it helps that it also has a superb brand cachet as the king of wood). I love turning kauri but sometimes you want a *challenge* (hah!)

And there are plenty of woods that give you that. They're hard, gnarly, oily, with cracks and splits and holes that make the chisel-work an interesting bareback ride at times. But that's part of the wonder of wood.

Some timbers smell – usually fragrantly but sometimes cloyingly so. Some timbers produce a toxic dust when you turn or sand them – rimu in New Zealand is one such culprit.

Some woods can break your heart; exposing insurmountable flaws as you delve down, or very occasionally, spontaneously shattering on the lathe because of hidden cracks and sudden, released timber tension.

It's the wonder of wood. Cabinetmakers don't experience this to my knowledge; their raw material is usually sawn and dressed and behaves itself. But turners often work with a lump of strange wood they've salvaged from a beach or forest and it may be totally unprocessed. And therein lies some of the excitement and fascination.

I want to also fly a flag here for the concept of recycling. Unlike house-builders, turners don't need very big bits of wood to do their thing. We can play with offcuts, discarded chunks, slabs too small for a table, old balustrades and posts – anything that's not rotten and is of a dimension to be clasped in a lathe.

When people chop down old trees, the wood generally ends up in the woodbox for next winter's fires – or out on the road, where drivers of a scavenging bent might load it into their boot for the same purpose. Fair enough. What else can you do with it? A lot of waste demolition timber still goes to landfill in New Zealand when it could be reused or repurposed, but old trees have limited on-use.

Except where turners are concerned. That old walnut or plum tree may seem like it has no new home after it's bowled by a cyclone but most turners would leap at the chance to get some of the trunk or branches. Both timbers are lovely for turning.

Your essential raw materials: wood blanks in varying stages of readiness from roughed out green bowls drying (bagged in shavings at top and upper right), to bandsawed rounds, chainsawed chunks and raw logs.

Piles of firewood chopped up by the road aren't always fit to turn though. They may have been split into too small a segment to do anything with, or be too weathered and fissured. But an eagle-eyed turner will always check the pile out – and will sometimes pick up a gem of a piece.

There are, of course, woods that aren't good, interesting or fun to turn at all. Too bland. Too soft or coarse-fibred. Too difficult to sand well or finish. *C'est la vie*.

There is something uplifting about taking an unwanted, dirty, shapeless, problematic hunk of wild wood and making something useful, decorative and polished from it. A tree has a finite life (it might be longer than ours but it's still finite) and it may simply rot back into the humus at the end of its life. But making something from it gives it a life beyond its own death – an element of utility and recognition for the simple, natural and often unique beauty finished wood has.

I love my turning, but I turn wood as much for the wood as for the turning. Turning metal has nothing like the same appeal – for me at least.

CHAPTER TWO: WOODTURNING EXPLAINED

OK. This is going to be the chapter where we get a bit technical and existing wood-turners may wish to skip it. In its simplest form, woodturning is a process where you clamp a suitable piece of wood to the rotating axle of a small motor mounted on a lathe. You then apply the edge of one of a set of special chisels to the rotating wood, resting the chisel on a metal toolrest. As the revolving wood turns past the tip of the chisel, the blade pares small curls of wood off.

That's the nub of the process. Putting aside some of the clever work advanced turners can do, in essence, everything you turn will be round or curved.

The Lathe

A typical lathe offers two modes of turning:

- An **open-ended mode** where the wood is fixed at one point on the axle of the motor – this is the way you make bowls, platters, vases.

- A **closed turning set-up**, known as turning between centres, where the wood is mounted between the spindle at the motor end (the headstock) and another point at the other end of the lathe bed – the tailstock (the way a pig is set up on a spit-roasting machine) and you turn along the length of the wood – typically for table and chair legs, candlesticks, pens and so on.

Lathes offer a range of speeds to rotate the wood; the bigger the hunk, the slower the speed and as you refine the shape you can increase the speed to remove the wood more quickly. Slow speeds are also advisable for hunks of wood that are asymmetrical; spin those suckers too fast and the whole shed will shake – and the wood might leap off and go on a demolition spree. That happened to me once. My half-completed rimu platter decided to reveal a major crack, the chisel dug in and the wood literally leapt off the lathe, missing me fortunately but taking out the fluorescent lamp in the ceiling of the garage and bouncing cleanly over the Honda CRV to pass out in the far corner. Yikes!

There are many different makes of lathes and as with any undertaking it pays to invest in a good model – "the bitterness of poor quality lingering long after the thrill of a cheap price..." as they say.

Right: My current set-up: a Teknatool Nova 3000 swivel-head with outboard arm (for large bowls and platters).

The lathe has a moveable toolrest which you position as close to the wood as possible. An option (which I took up) to enable larger works to be handled at the open-end is an outrigger toolrest.

My first lathe was a pretty crude and limited model – I can't even remember the make – but I learnt the basics on it and in time got a much better one – an early Teknatool, which elevated my turning to a new

level. I later upgraded to a Teknatool with a swivel head, which gives so much more flexibility (*see photograph*) to turn on the open end. My lathes have all been secondhand and a good one is reasonably affordable. Or if you're flush, you might go the whole hog and get one of the fancy new (well they've been around a while I guess) direct-drive lathes where there are no gears and pulleys you have to move around to change the lathe speed – you just turn a dial to speed it up, which is great, but possibly a little scary. Like having a turbo engine and massive horsepower in a car. Take care.

Mounting the wood

Wood is attached to the motor axle using either a face-plate or a chuck (open-ended turning) or small devices called centres that pin the wood at either end (spindle turning).

A face-plate is a flat disc with a thread that attaches to the axle; you screw the faceplate to the wood.

A chuck is a mechanical clamp which can be adjusted to "grab" the wood, usually via a spigot or dovetail you've turned on the wood (using the faceplate).

On the closed end you pin the piece of wood between what are called centres – small devices that hold the wood between the headstock and the tailstock and enabling it to spin freely.

Pictured right are two chucks – a set of Cole Jaws (larger) and a Teknatool Nova chuck (lower right), along with two faceplates and assorted tools to tighten the chucks.

Chisels

The chisel is the core tool in turning; connecting the turner to the wood the way a paintbrush connects the artist to his/her canvas. Chisels essentially provide a sharp, stabilised (by the toolrest) edge that the wood slides past shedding dust and tendrils of timber to arrive at the shape you're seeking.

Most chisels have a bevel – an angled face at the cutting tip that the turner aims to "rest" on the wood surface during turning. Bevels come at specified angles aligned with what sort of cutting you're trying to do. A move of the hands will engage the cutting edge by the bevel but it's a delicate skill best honed by gentle practice at low speeds.

Turners use a range of chisels to cut the wood away and progressively finish the work to the point where sanding is the next step.

Chisels are to the turner what woods (hah), irons and putters are to the golfer. The golfer draws the club out of the bag depending on what stage of the hole he is at: a driver at the tee, irons – progressively shorter – down the fairway, pitching wedges or sandirons around the green, and a putter on it – to finish off the hole.

Turners also begin big and get progressively finer in the tool they use. Their "golf bag" is likely to include:

- **Roughing-out chisels** – specially for the early stages of shaping the block of wood, big and designed for the jolts and buffets you'll get when apply the chisel to an uneven surface turning around
- **Bowl-shaping chisels or gouges** – my favourite chisels, since I turn almost exclusively items like bowls and platters at the open-end of the lathe; these have a deep flute at the tip of the chisel creating a semi-circular cutting edge and they come in varying sizes
- **Scraping chisels** – not always favoured by turning purists, scraping chisels are used to remove fine imperfections and ridges in the turning surface, usually at a later stage in the process
- **Spindle-turning chisels** (for turning between centres, e.g. a table leg) – these include a gouge like a bowl gouge but with a shallower flute and skew chisels which tend to be broader and with a straight cutting edge on an angle – used for removing wood and turning small features on the work

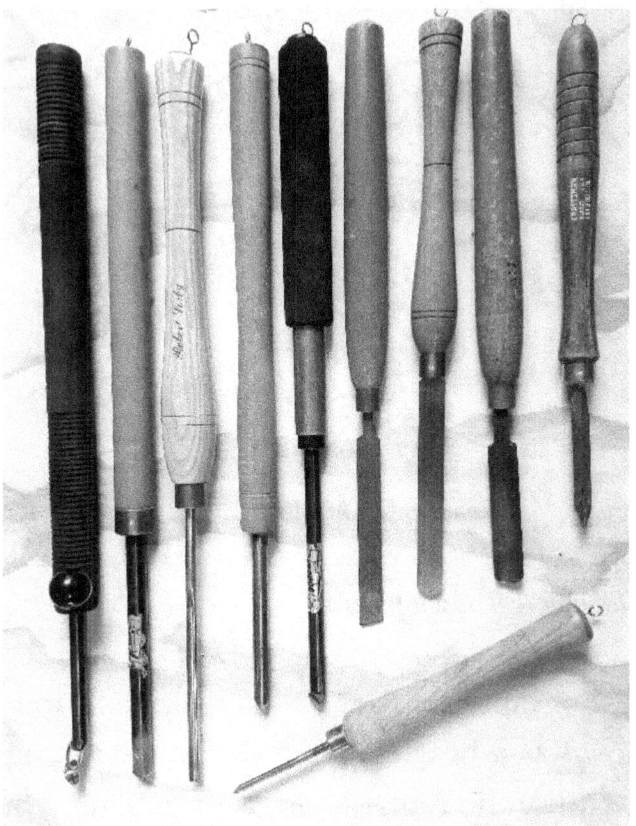

Pictured: my line-up, which includes (from left) a Woodcut hollowing tool, a large bowl gouge, a smaller bowl gouge, an in-between bowl gouge, a ring-tool, a skew chisel, a scraping chisel, a roughing-out chisel, a parting tool and, at bottom, a fine gouge for making spigots and beads.

- **Specialised chisels** – in the bag you're also likely to find a parting tool, used to "cut off" a work you've completed between centres, and there may be other chisels that perform a particular finishing role, often homemade by the turner with a little steel-working ability.

Over time you kind of develop a bond with your chisels; you get to know them well, their good (and bad) points, their little peculiarities. But they age like we do and after many years of use and sharpening may run out of steel, especially those with a flute, and you have to "retire" them (though perhaps reusing the handles).

Some chisels come with an interchangeable tip arrangement; when the tip wears out you just replace it – not the whole chisel.

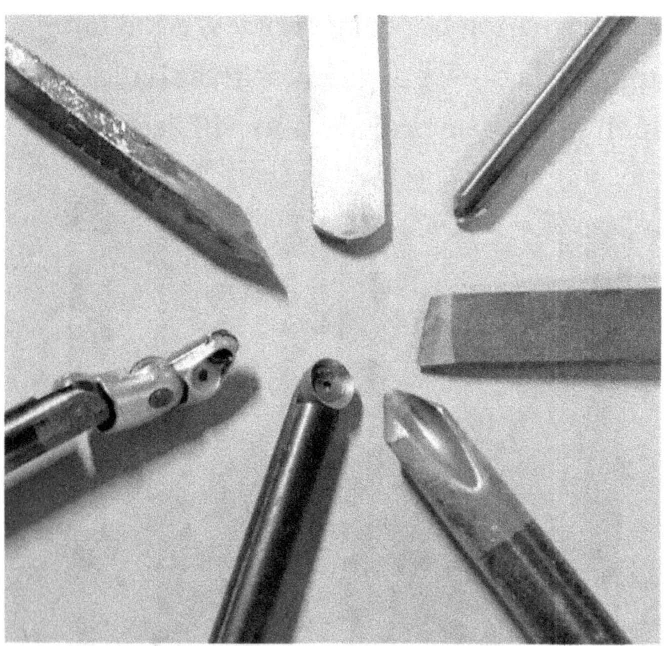

Some turners also like making (turning) their own handles out of a wood they like, in a style or shape they prefer. It's all part of the fun.

But invest well in your chisels and look after them; they are the key to the game.

Above: Close-up of some chisel tips, clockwise from 12 – a rounded scraper, a small bowl gouge, a small skew chisel, a large bowl gouge with replaceable tip, a ring chisel, a hollowing tool and a parting tool.

Not quite a chisel but worth a mention in the same breath is what's known as a **bowl-saver.** This is a cunning device that you can use to maximise the return from a large blank you're turning into a bowl. All the wood you scoop out of the inside of the bowl is generally wasted and it may have been of a dimension to support one or even two more progressively smaller bowls – the way Russian dolls sit inside each other.

With a bowl-saver, you can scoop out those smaller bowls intact – and incidentally save a lot of turning and thus maximise the return, particularly if you're a commercial turner, from what may be a particularly fine piece of kauri or walnut. In doing so you can also create a set of matching bowls. Well worth looking into.

Other equipment

Turners can make something with a basic lathe, chuck/faceplate and chisels, but most - if not all - eventually (depending on the state of their wallet) add a few other items of equipment to their turning shed.

Grinder

A simple bench grinder is a must really, since those chisels have to be kept sharp. The difference between a sharp chisel and a dull/blunt one can be a lot of grief. Some woods are tough, and blunt won't (ahem) cut the mustard so to speak. Hone the blade well and all but the most iron-like woods will come around. Usually you go for a white stone on the grinder too as opposed to the coarser, grey grinding wheels. Another indispensable adjunct to the grinding operation is some form of "jig" to hold the chisel as you hone the edge and bevel – the jig can be adjusted to the right angle for the bevel.

Pictured: my Carbatec grinder with white wheel on the right and a Woodcut chisel-sharpening jig mounted on the base.

You can get by with files or handheld honing tools but a good grinder does the trick much more accurately and quickly.

Bandsaws and other saws

A **bandsaw** is an optional accessory; it's essentially a tool for shaping the blanks of wood before you mount them. Where possible, you aim to cut away the wood that is surplus to the shape of your item. Making a blank (the raw piece of wood ready for mounting on the lathe) the aim is to have it cut out in the circular size you want, or with any large, excess, protruding bits cut off.

A handsaw or fretsaw will do the same, just a lot more slowly and labour-intensively; a table saw or reciprocating saw are other options and a small electric **chainsaw** can be used for rougher cuts. I'll touch on the health and safety of the whole turning journey in a later chapter but a word here about each of the sawing devices thus far referenced – be *very* careful in their use. They will all reduce your piano-playing options considerably with a moment's inattention - or considerably liven up the A&E department at your local hospital if it's a quiet day.

Dust extractors and fans

I'll talk more about dust in the aforementioned H&S chapter – it is a big issue – and so while a specialized **dust extractor** is also an optional extra, if, in the course of your turning journey, you can afford one, it's worth considering. It's basically a large vacuum cleaner (and I use mine that way all the time) which can capture the dust and wood curls and haul them into a storage bag which you need to empty periodically. If you have a neighbour that likes composting for their garden they may be interested in the contents.

Another weapon in the war on dust is some form of **fan**; as you turn, you can position it behind you to blow the turning spillage away from you and the lathe – possibly out an open door or window (into an area of the property where accumulating dust isn't an issue or can be readily collected). Get my drift? Sorry, couldn't resist that pun.

Vacuum cleaner

If you don't have a dust extractor, a simple vacuum cleaner is handy for the temple. You will produce prodigious amounts of dust and wood curls in your turning; the actual volume ending up on the floor defies credibility when you consider the relatively small volume of actual dense wood you've removed. But that's wood for you. Some turners don't mind the accumulated shavings on the floor or the shed but I tend to keep it under control from a (fire) safety perspective.

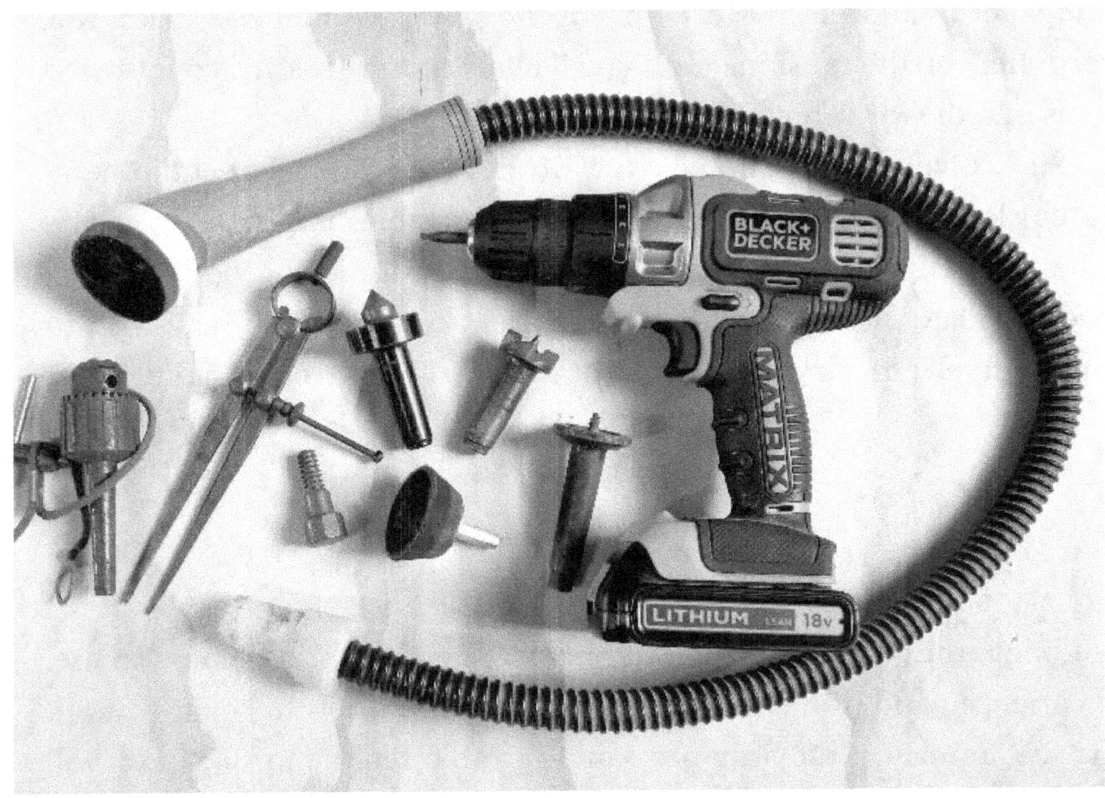

Pictured: Some of the key bench items to aid the turning journey: an electric drill with a Velcro sanding attachment, a number of "centres" for use in spindle turning, calipers to scribe the circle that will be your e.g. bowl circumference, a couple of screw chucks, and coiled around the group is Rene Baxalle's vacuum sanding tool.

Power drill

I'm picking most people contemplating get into turning will have a power drill. It'll get plenty of use on the turning journey. You'll use the screwdriver (Phillips mainly) attachments to screw the faceplates to the wood and often the drill bits to make holes for the screws, though I use self-tapping screws almost exclusively and only have to drill holes occasionally in some of the very hard timbers, like puriri.

You'll also find the power drill handy for sanding the turned article (generally on the lathe), using those small attachments that have a rubber sanding pad with Velcro surfacing to hold small circular pieces of sandpaper (mandrells). More on finishing later in the book, but a few words here on the finishing tools you'll likely acquire to turn your turned items into the (breathless) finished product.

Should you have gathered a few of these extra items of equipment, it'll be clear that you have quite a few power cables in proximity to the lathe, so it's wise to invest in some form of multi-plug box that will accommodate them all and help keep them orderly. You may wish to consult an electrician friend on what the best setup from a safety point of view is.

Sanding

Sanding is the part of turning where you expend the most elbow grease. Experienced and professional turners use their chisels to get as smooth and fine a finish as they can pre-sanding and often the turned work will actually require a relatively small amount of actual sanding before the oils and/or waxes are applied.

But for the rest of us mere mortals, there's usually a heap of sanding to do. So, you need a range of sandpapers which are graded according to their fineness or coarseness, based on the grit that forms the sanding surface. Conventionally, you start with a coarse grade (my starter grade is 80 grit); you then work your way through the likes of 100, 120, 180,

220, 280, 320 and 400 grit. Some turners keep going finer than that to maybe 1200. After 400 you're getting into wet n dry sandpaper terrain; I hardly ever use a liquid (oil or water) with my sanding of turned items but some turners do. Your call, in time.

Sanding blocks or the drill-mounted Velcro pad setups are part of the game too. And there's another great device I'd recommend for your armoury: a sanding attachment like the rubber Velcro pad for the drill but this time with a hose attached that you connect to a vacuum (made by North Shore turner Rene Baxalle). The sandpaper discs you attach to the Velcro pad  have three small holes in them (*or four on the larger model pictured above, along with two smaller mandrells*) that enable dust to be sucked from the word as you sand it. The head of this device rotates too, picking up on the action of the lathe (you sand with the wood spinning) and in doing so avoid an issue with simply sanding the turning wood – scratch rings from the sandpaper. A priceless addition.

I'll dwell more on how you sand in chapter 9. This chapter is more about the gear you need – essentials and optionals.

The other two *absolutely* indispensable items you'll need on hand constantly, as you turn, are facemasks and protective glasses.

Masks come in all price brackets and there are ones for dust (and separate ones for fumes – see below on finishing). Get the best you can. There's a good one available in New Zealand that's washable which is a good economy.

Protective glasses also come in a range of styles and prices. As you turn, dust and wood can fly off the chisel towards the eyes, nose, ears (and clothing pockets) and cause discomfort or health issues – so always turn with glasses on if you can. Wearing a mask with glasses can lead to fogging of the glass but experiment with the positioning till you eliminate that issue.

Many turners invest in full protective helmets, often with filtration and battery-powered aeration to reduce fogging and avoid breathing dusty air. I had one once but found it a bit heavy and hot in the New Zealand summer. Your call.

Finishing

You finish the turned and sanded item for two reasons: to enhance its look (and feel) and to protect it.

There are a host of finishes, and preferences vary among turners as to what works best; in time, again, you will settle on your preferred mode of finishing and products to use. My account will suggest what I found worked (and it differs for different timbers) but it's not definitive in any way.

Finishing can be challenging for two reasons: one, it may not always do justice to the wonderful grain and figure you've revealed; and two – it's a fume-y game. Ventilation of the temple is essential when you're finishing – at least where some of the products you may use are concerned.

Most turners use oils and waxes and there are a range of these around:

- **Danish oil** – This is popular and works with most woods; a mix of Tung oil and other ingredients. My go-to.
- **Tung oil** – Also popular on its own.
- **Linseed oil** – Often mixed with turpentine; still popular (I've never used it).
- **Carnauba wax** – Used to impart a lustre to the finished product; may be used on top of oil; quite hard.
- **Beeswax** – The other common wax used; quite soft. Some wax products combine both carnauba and beeswax.
- **Sanding sealer** – This is a great product, but it sets/dries fast; you buff it back with a bit of very fine steel wool. You can oil over it

(and/or wax) but I find it often does the finishing trick on its own (with 2-3 coats).

Other finishes

Many advanced turners bring a range of other finishes to the turning game, embellishing the wood with stains, colours, resins, "blonding" products, wire, string or whatever they fancy to arrive at the artistic effect they're seeking.

I occasionally use a little shell or resin but tend to let the wood speak

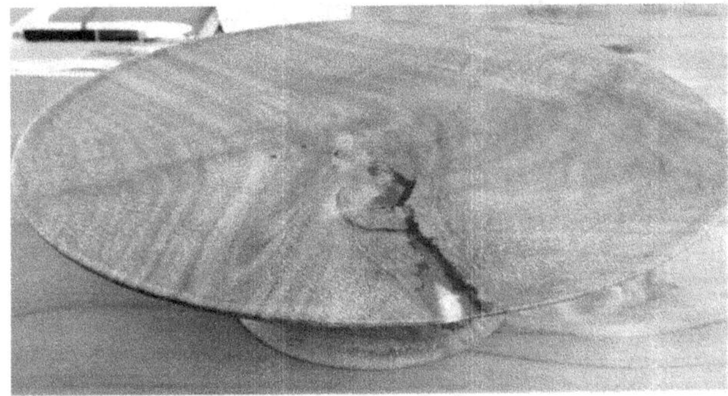

for itself. Each to their own. There's no right answer where personal preference or taste is concerned. If you arrive at something you and your audience or market find beautiful...then it's beautiful.

Above: This honeysuckle cake-stand had a significant crack that I filled with clear resin and incorporated a small wentle shell.

Here's another trick woodturners use. Wood often has small cracks that can't be turned away without reducing the wood to the point where it ceases to be shapeable. Cracks by their nature can also grow, extend and possibly lead to a part of the turned item breaking off.

But you can repair cracks, and the way many woodturners (myself included) tidy up and strengthen a cracked bit of the wood is through super glue – and wood dust. As you turn your wood, you will accumulate a lot of fine dust around the lathe and the trick is to scrape that dust up and store it in a small ziplock plastic bag, with the name of the wood on the outside. Over time you build up a collection of the various wood dusts.

To repair the crack, you carefully squirt a small amount of super glue along it, and quickly pour/push/scrape dust into the glue (with a screwdriver or penknife – not your fingers...super glue is not forgiving where skin is concerned) to create a slurry. You let it dry (not long) and then sand it back; the glue and dust should have bound the sides of the crack together and the blemish will not be too noticeable given the dust imparts something of the colouration of the wood.

If you're finishing, you'll need a steady source of rags: cotton is best, cut into handkerchief sizes or smaller. You use rags to apply oil (or a brush can be used) and wax, and to wipe and buff the oiled or waxed wood. Used rags should be disposed of carefully.

There is of course a little and growing sensitivity about the use of oils on turned items that might be used with food. My understanding is that once an item is oiled and the oil has dried it's relatively safe to convey food. Some oils, however, provide the reassurance that they are food suitable – one of the industry's doyens, the very personable, energetic Whangarei-based turner and teacher Shane Hewitt has one. More about Shane later.

Where food is concerned, it's worth noting that wooden bowls and platters don't go well with liquids which can seep into the timber and spoil it. The odd splash won't hurt but if you use a bowl for salads it pays to wipe it clean and dry soon after use, and it's OK from time to time to wipe the bowl with a little salad oil (not peanut oil which can leave a rancid smell).

Over time, interestingly, the simple act of handling bowls with (surprise) your hands does impart a bit of a patina to the bowl (from the oil and moisture on your fingers) which adds to the charm and does no harm.

Lighting

A word about lighting. It goes without saying that you need to see what you're doing so your temple needs good illumination. That might be no worries during the day when you perhaps have excellent windows to the outside world and sun streams in. But at night, artificial lighting has to take over. A good ceiling light will give you the main coverage but you may also want to invest in some additional spot-lighting that you can direct onto the surface you are turning, so you can see how you're doing, what grooves and ridges need to be smoothed out and what the grain is looking like. Those relatively cheap student lamps (*see photo right*) that have clips aren't bad – easy to move around and affix somewhere.

Once your lathe is mounted on the bench and you gauge what lighting you have already, you can make a call on how you might need to supplement it.

Clothing

Finally, a sartorial note. Turning is dusty and can be a bit messy, oils and waxes-wise. So, don't wear you best bib 'n tucker. Anything with open pockets will fill with dust and shavings. Long, loose sleeves may be caught in the spinning lathe. But t-shirts and shorts are fine, though be prepared to end up covered in shavings and dust – the chisel angles sometimes unavoidably jet the stuff straight at you, like the plume from a snow-making machine. Hence the importance of facial protection.

Covered shoes may be wise in case you drop a chisel. There are special high-collared turner's smocks available which shed dust and stop it going down the neck of a top; not a bad idea as many cloths hook shavings like velcro.

Once you're a seasoned turner, it's a pretty relaxed game. Dress comfortably and enjoy that.

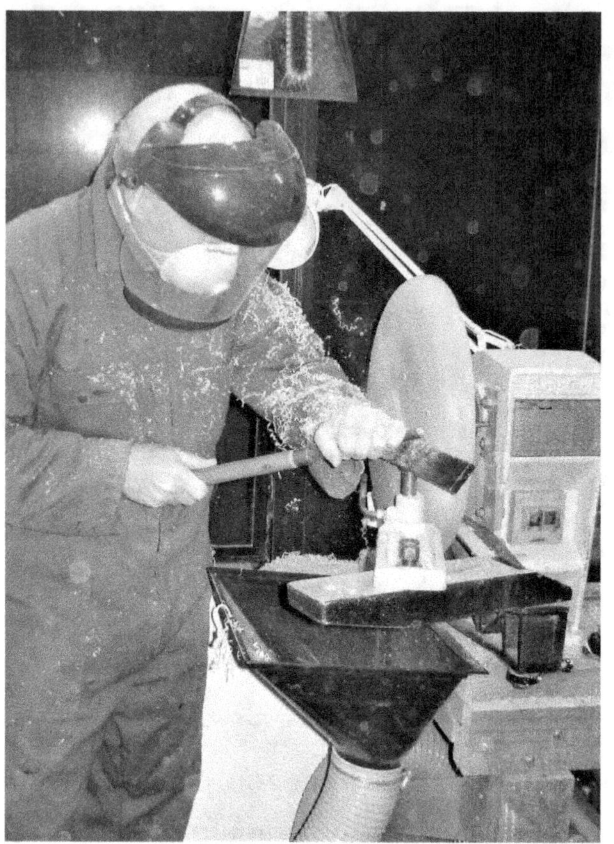

Must be winter – full overalls on. This in the early days (the lathe is my first Teknatool); I later cut the sleeves off the overalls at the elbow to avoid snagging. Note the light in the background with the reticulating arm – very handy for illuminating that inner space in a deep bowl.

So that's the world of turning. As I said, this book isn't intended to be just another guide to how to turn – there are plenty of excellent such guides around – but I wanted to sketch in the main basic details and in chapter 9 I'll walk you through a couple of typical turning projects in more detail.

But now let's turn (hah) to the crux of this book – the meditative dimension of turning.

CHAPTER THREE: TURNING AND MEDITATION

The last chapter was more for meditators who didn't know much about turning; this one is the obverse – for those who don't know much about meditation (but *may* be a turner).

Or perhaps both worlds are slightly alien to you. In which case, twice welcome, friend.

There are many many books around about meditation, along with websites, courses, articles galore, teachers and advocates from all walks of life. I have a phone app that times my meditations with a series of gentle gongs and bells, and it proudly tells me, when I tune in, how many people are meditating (using the app) globally right now, how many so far today, and where they are on a map of the world. It's a significant number.

Meditation is a phenomenon that has moved from the world of Buddhism into the mainstream. It has corporate creds and celebrity backers. New Age, come-of-age. Health studies abound showing the benefits of meditation for a range of health disorders.

But plenty of people still have no idea of what it is, how it works, or what is does. It has abiding "black art" status. And many people try it and give up because "it doesn't seem to work".

So, what is it? I'll answer this from (again) my own experience because I am not a trained meditation teacher (just as I'm not a professional turner). I'm probably not even a very advanced meditator – the kind that can go hours, days, even weeks "in meditation" on a retreat, often in silence. Maybe one day...but for the moment I'm a 15-minute-a-day, maybe twice-a-day, meditator...and I miss the occasional day.

But that's meditation. It's a challenge to keep it as an enduring habit. It should be regular but sometimes it's hard to cement the regular daily spot.

Maybe 30 years ago I took up yoga, principally as a form of exercise when I was recovering from a stomach operation that scissored me from navel to sternum. Quite a scar and took a while to heal all those severed chest and belly muscles. It came after I had a duodenal ulcer bleed, so the yoga was a double balm: gentle exercise to reacquaint those ruptured muscles with movement, and some calm stuff for the mind while I figured how to be less demanding of myself (source of the ulcer).

Yoga, as you may know, is part flexibility and joint exercise (Pilates-plus), part breathing practices and part meditation and relaxation. I fell in love with it (and most yoga teachers since) when my first night-class instructor told us "This is *your* time; put aside everything that happened today and all that you're thinking about that's coming up - and enjoy the next 90 minutes."

Of those 90-minute sessions, the last 30 minutes was relaxation. Stretched and squeezed and warmed-up after an hour of *asanas* (poses) and *pranayama* (breathing exercises), we lay down in *sivasana* (the ill-named but sublime "corpse" pose) and our yogi began talking us into a calm, meditative space...gently summoning us from it half an hour later.

That was my first intro' to meditation though I didn't know (or call it that) at the time.

Later, I formally (well, through a book) taught myself how to enter, if fleetingly, that zone where the mind simplifies its activity down, shutting out most - if not all - the thoughts, random or otherwise, that come and go perpetually while we are mentally active. Or trying to shut them out.

Meditation in simple terms

My understanding of meditation is that, in its simplest basic form, it is about:

- sitting down, usually cross-legged, somewhere warm, not brightly lit and quiet, where you won't be disturbed
- possibly sitting on a cushion to cushion your butt cheeks and help keep the back straight
- usually gently closing your eyes and placing your hands on your lap or knees
- setting a timer or having a watch handy to track the allotted time (which can be anything you like – my current number is 15 minutes)
- settling into a regular breathing pattern, perhaps deeper and slower
- then finding a focus – something you will concentrate the mind on – while you try to gently corral the thoughts that are flitting about your mind.

And in that last bullet-point is the crux of meditation. The mind is really a wild animal where thoughts are concerned. They arise out of nowhere – lots of them – and career around the head while you try to keep order. Meditators call it "the monkey mind". You feel like a teacher in a classroom where the kids are all talking at once and racing around throwing stuff. You can bring order to it, but such is the mind it can suddenly erupt into random discourse at any moment, as you're distracted by some stimuli, dwell on something from the past, or a future concern or event.

Meditation is about trying to gain control of the classroom again; rein in the monkeys.

It's not about emptying the mind of all thoughts – well, not as I understand anyway, though some advanced yogis may well head for that space. Instead it is about recognising that thought-barrage and keeping it at bay while you focus on that simple thing that is the centre of your meditative practice. A yoga teacher somewhere along the way described it memorably as being like "gently pushing away those little children coming up and interrupting you".

For many, me included, that "simple thing" is your slow, steady breath, which, yoga-style, is through the nostrils. You aid the focus – in

my case at least – in two ways: by counting the breaths and by visualising the breath coming in and leaving, perhaps focusing on the sensation of it crossing your top lip. What you count to and how long you count for is up to you – whatever works. Many count to 10, then start again...and repeat that for as long as they wish (or can). I count up to my age (62 at time

of writing) – and back down again to 0. The count provides a focus and a task. If you suddenly find some monkey thoughts have slid in and the count has stopped, you acknowledge this and – no judgements here – resume the count, from the start again, if you really want to be tough.

That doesn't use up 15 minutes in my case, so I accompany the breathing in my head with a mantra that is commonly used in meditation – "so-hum". You think/say "so" on the intake and "hum" on the out-breath. You may choose another phrase to repeat – your call. But it's the small anchor to your meditation.

Other focuses people use include a candle flame or a meaningful (but not complicated) picture or a mandala perhaps. The point is to have something that you hold to and follow for the allotted time, at the same time (should you need to) gently acknowledging ("I see you – now go away") those random thoughts that elbow in – and dismissing them. Without judgement or emotion.

I also have time if the count goes well (it doesn't always) to do a little affirming. I acknowledge the things I'm lucky to have like reasonably good health (for the moment), close friends and family; I also go through my Stoicism code – the four R's of what is Right (good), what is Real (actual), what is "Ropable" (controllable) - and the importance of being Resilient. For good measure, I tick off a few important abstract notions (also part of the Stoic's playlist) to try to hold on to – Strength, Love, Wisdom, Justice, Courage and Self-discipline.

By about then a wooden gong tells me the 15 minutes is up. A few yogic stretches and I resume the day's proceedings.

It is quite hard to nail it as I described above. Some days, the monkey mind is almost unmanageable. And beginning meditators get discouraged; they can't do it, they say/think. And give up. It doesn't work for them, they believe.

Wrong. Simply *trying* to meditate is success in itself. Stopping somewhere quiet for five minutes and breathing slowly is a "win" all of its own. The breakthrough, though it may not feel like it to a novice, is in getting a count going and having a go at pushing those thoughts away. Realising from this position of quiet observation that this little process is happening in your head and you're kind of in charge...much of the time...or now and then!

Like Yoga, meditation isn't a competition where you only have a few medallists. *Try* it and you win. But, in saying that, you have to keep going with the practice and make it as much of a regular habit as you can.

A few thoughts here on the handmaiden to meditation these days – called mindfulness. The word mindful is a fairly old-fashioned one: "be mindful how you go on the walk" (i.e. be careful). The opposite of mindless? But it has come to stand for a state of just dwelling on the moment: the snippet of nature you're observing; that piece of fruit you're eating; that music you're hearing. Enjoying it – and not fretting on the past or future. Noticing what's about you more than being internally obsessed with a myriad mental distractions. Taking time to smell the flowers.

Hard to do – we're all busy people – but worth trying from time to time.

OK, that's Meditation 101 according to RM. But clearly there wasn't a lathe in sight there. What is Murray on about?

Let's go back to the core purpose of meditation. To calm and simplify the thinking and strengthen your ability to control your thoughts. To focus the mind for a while.

Sitting for 15 minutes isn't the only way to achieve that. People do walking meditations in the forest or on beaches. Practised meditators can do it on a bus, shutting out the hubbub around them.

Meditative pursuits

Some recreational pursuits have meditation DNA through and through.

Several years ago, I did a little PR for a friend who ran a stamp collecting business. He'd buy and sell stamps and his clients included a lot of surgeons he told me. Being a surgeon is an intense and stressful occupation; often, at your fingertips, are life-and-death situations. You spend hours in an operating theatre, where a slip, or something you miss, can have awful consequences.

My client said many surgeons turned to stamp collecting because they could go into the study, pull out a book or box of stamps and with tweezers and a magnifying glass, peruse and admire or sort and research these beautiful miniature works of art at their leisure for hours - and think of nothing else. A meditative practice if ever I heard of one.

...like woodturning

And so to turning – and this may be true of many crafts.

You break free of a busy and perhaps stressful day, where everyone wants a piece of you – positively or negatively. You escape the office for the sanctuary of home and maybe there's plenty bubbling away there to distract or perturb you.

So you make for the garage/shed, the temple.

You prepare a blank for turning – or there's one already on the lathe.

You get the lighting right, the ventilation, a fan going maybe.

You check the chisels you're going to use. Nice 'n sharp? Tune 'em up if not.

Then – curtain up – you set the lathe going and start turning. At this point you can't afford to let your mind wander. You have to watch the tip of the chisel as it does its work and know when to subtly twist and turn the handle to finesse your cut.

Depending on where you are in the stage of the project, there is a start point and an end point (of the stage). So you're keeping tabs on that. Time passes. An hour, two maybe – and you've made significant progress; perhaps gone  from rough chunk of wood to completion of the outside of your bowl.

You take it off the lathe and remount to hollow out the inside.

It's you and the chisel and the wood and the hum of the lathe. No mobile phone. No TV. No dishes. Your focus has been on a postage-stamp-sized space 20-50 centimetres from your eyes. For two hours or more. And a work of art is slowly forming under your rapt gaze. Tell me that's not a meditative experience. It is for me.

Turning is not just a functional gig to rest your mind though; it is (or has the potential to become) a strongly abiding passion. It's a refuge. A distraction from the mad world. It's magical. It's raw. It's silky. It's frustrating at times.

It's also a journey – every single time you turn you take a new slightly different little path. It's exploration. It's restorative and creative. It's revelation (along the way and at the final unveiling). It's fulfilling. It's giving.

It's wood and chisels and speed and mess. It can be dirty, dusty, noisy. Or whisper-sweet as the oil does its magic.

It's one anchor to a satisfying life – at least for me.

In the 1998 movie *The Horse Whisperer* (from the book by Nicholas Evans of the same name), Robert Redford plays a man who has the gift of being able to tame wild or troubled horses by gently talking to them and being enormously patient – a horse whisperer. I liken the woodturner's role to horse-whispering – call it wood-whispering if you like.

When you mount a piece of rough wood – particularly where it's not a cleanly cut, circular, even blank - it's a little like that wild horse. It will buck and bellow and jerk the chisel around for a while – and set the bench (or even the whole shed) rocking and rolling too, but as you patiently and firmly persist with your cutting pattern, in time it calms down, becomes more even (tempered) and behaves well on the lathe.

Like Redford did, you take the wild thing to a point where it's refined and graceful. Calm.

You might be rolling your eyes at this point (what *did* Murray get up to in the 1960s?!) but indulge me. You know I like my analogies, and this is intended to be a spiritual book more than an engineering one.

But let's also step outside that actual turning experience to the other concentric circles radiating out from it. Turning is exercise. It also takes organisation so it's a mental (and planning) discipline.

It is a pastime you can turn to at any time 24/7. You don't have to travel to do it. There are competitions but you don't have to compete…just do.

There are clubs you can join and develop lasting friendships through; or it can be a solitary pursuit.

You *can* start a project, leave it on the lathe for a month and come back to it and resume like you never left. My gurus (see later chapters) would suggest this approach has its downside…wood does tend to "wander" if untended for long. But you're not chained to the lathe.

It is creative. As your skills develop, the variety of what you can achieve in the type of item, size, shape, and finish, just grows.

Every item has the potential to be unique, a one-off. You can sell them. You can gift them. You can collect them. And giving them away is nice to do. You leave the recipient with a piece of you – some sweat certainly, blood maybe, tears rarely…

But that's the bonus; making them is the prize.

A lifeline in retirement

I want to expand this particular thread of the book for a moment. Psychologists and sociologists, community workers and geriatricians will all have stories of people who led busy, successful rewarding lives where they were masters of their calling and garnered broad respect and perhaps fame.

They reached retirement, however, and it all fell apart. Not working, they were bored; they may have had plenty of money, and the world offers many enticements to take it off your hands. But they didn't have an abiding calling in their retirement years. Their sense of achievement progressively dwindled and perhaps their mental and physical health declined.

Those savvy enough to foresee this happening usually try to put in place something productive in their lives to maintain a sense of purpose and connection. Perhaps a continuation of what they were doing but in a more relaxed, part-time, possibly *pro-bono* capacity. Or they take a hobby they dabbled in occasionally while fully employed and make it a more pervasive pursuit in their lives.

I recall many years ago as a journalist at Mount Maunganui doing a story on a Tauranga man Harry Highet (*below*), a civil engineer who in 1923 had invented a small (2.13m) class of yacht – a sailing dinghy really – called the P Class (or Tauranga Class, after the harbour at The Mount where he perfected his design). The P Class opened up yachting (and its competitive possibilities) for generations of young sailors, girls and boys, who cut their early sailing teeth on these simple, tiny, sole-handed yachtettes. Many went on to compete at higher levels including national representation – like the late Sir Peter Blake and Sir Russell Coutts.

When I called around to Harry's house to interview him, he was in his mid-90s and while he was expecting me and I was on time, when I knocked on his door, no one answered. I thought he might be in the

garden so popped my head around the corner and spotted him in the lounge watching TV with a large set of headphones on. I caught his attention and the interview proceeded and I found him to be a thoroughly...peaceful is the best word...man. A gentleman in every sense. He didn't sail any more of course but he remained active in a captivating way. Down in his basement he showed me his workshop where he made wooden toys – trucks, cars, graders and the like, which he carefully cut out, assembled and painted – then gave away to whatever charity might want them for needy children at Christmas.

It was a profound moment for me. I thought: How satisfying that must be, to be still giving, using your expertise at such an age.

Harry died in 1989 only a few years short of 100. But he left his mark in so many ways. That's something to aspire to.

CHAPTER FOUR: CREATING THE TEMPLE

In chapter 2, I noted the items of equipment turning is built around. But it all has to be housed somewhere. A shed or the back of a garage is the usual location.

I also mentioned lighting in chapter 2; natural is good but you may be turning more often in the evening, after work or after dinner, so good lighting is essential.

The centre of the operation is your lathe which may be up to a metre long and certainly you need to allow around 700mm, probably more if you're going to turn long items like chair legs or banisters.

The bench it's mounted on needs to be solid. Many lathes come with their own stand – possibly solid cast-iron. When the lathe is turning with a large item on it, particularly if the item is asymmetrical, the stand might jump around a bit unless it's bolted down or weighed down with sandbags or bricks.

I have my lathe positioned on the left-hand end of a 600mm x 1500mm, four-ply kitset bench, which works fine. It can be up against a wall or in a corner, but there should be standing space both to the left hand (short) side and in front of the long side.

The floor shouldn't be too hard or cold; you'll be standing on it for long periods at a time. Use some form of mat – rubber or textile is advisable - but ensure it won't slip.

You should have your regular tools close at hand. I have a bench behind me with the grinder on it. My dust extractor is to the left of the bench when I'm turning. I also have a two-metre shelf behind me where all my wood is stored. My tools are on the wall directly behind the lathe (in front of me as I turn). I have small eyelets in the end of my chisels so I can hang them off hooks, in descending order of size.

Then you just have to settle on where your various other tools are. Your call again. In time you'll work out the best locations arising from your pattern of use. Cupboards and drawers are handy since you can close them off; otherwise dust gets into everything. You vacuum a lot in this game – unless you're happy to grow a bed of shavings around your feet (which can be a fire risk).

If you want to control your dust, having a movable fan on hand is worth considering. I have one mounted on a stand at about shoulder height that I position behind me and turn on with the door opposite open, so dust and shavings are blown away from me and the turning area.

In your happy place...

You'll need a secure cupboard away from electrics and the grinder – for your oils and waxes, which can be highly flammable. I'll touch on this more in the H&S chapter to follow.

Your rag bin should also be handy. Likewise your rubbish bin.

Lathes, drills, vacuums, grinders and the like can make a reasonable din, so some sound-proofing may be warranted – or just decent separation from others in the family needing peace and quiet, or neighbours who don't like machine noise. Generally, the level isn't high.

It goes without saying that you'll need power, and a sink nearby may be useful to wash dusty or oily hands.

One useful item to have on the wall close by is a small whiteboard you can sketch your shapes on, though a pad is fine if space is limited.

And decorate the temple. If you become an avid turner, you'll spend a fair bit of time in the temple so have a few pictures, knick-knacks or memorabilia around. Get some ambience going!

Every temple needs its votive offerings – make what you will of this eclectic collection!

CHAPTER FIVE: STAYING SAFE

Thus far through the book I've scattered the odd bit of health and safety advice where turning is concerned, but hopefully this chapter will consolidate the safety messages and resonate.

Any spinning motor brings risks. In turning, the risk is magnified by the often-hefty chunk of wood attached to the motor which may be going around at 570rpm or more. That's quick. You're manoeuvring a sharp tool against that spinning object and cutting into it. It's attached to the lathe but can sometimes come loose. Get the chisel in the wrong position and the lathe can kick it abruptly in your direction.

Turners refer to "dig-ins" where wrong positioning of the chisel means that the sharp chisel tip gouges into the wood, which is usually more damaging to the wood than the turner but can still give you a bit of a shock.

Right: A classic dig-in; the chisel tip goes too obliquely, starts tunnelling and suddenly you get a major gouge (or, worse, the bowl also snaps off its spigot and bounces around the bench like this one did).

Developing the right techniques for mounting the wood and making the turning cuts will reduce the risk considerably, but even the best have the occasional lapse – a wake-up call to avoid complacency.

As noted, a spinning motor can also "grab" loose items like cords, clothing and long hair and mess you up in seconds. Mitigate the risk if you can. The hair gods solved the latter issue for me many years ago.

All the equipment you use that relies on electricity poses a risk of electric shocks if the wiring is damaged, so ensure your leads, plugs and power points are all fit-for-use. Drills and saws, especially electric ones, can also make a mess of a hand or leg if an accident occurs, so take extra care in their use. A first-aid kit in the temple makes sense. If you have a chainsaw, make sure you have protective gear on when you use it: glasses or helmet, gloves, earmuffs, hard-capped boots - and leather chaps aren't a bad idea.

Pictured: full-face protective visor, ear-muffs, safety glasses, three types of mask and heavy gloves (for wood-handling and chainsawing).

As you turn you will generate large amounts of dust and shavings – perfect tinder for a fire. Don't have any open flames in the temple and keep on top of the accumulating dust.

Grinders create sparks so keep the dust and any finishing materials away from the grinding operation. Likewise watch those finishing rags. Don't leave them lying around; dispose of them as soon as you've finished with them. I'm told they can spontaneously combust (yikes!) though it's never happened to me...touch wood.

So those are some of the external physical hazards.

Possibly the trickiest H&S issue in turning, which I suspect leads some turners to eventually give the game away, is dust getting into the respiratory system. Turning in general, and sanding in particular, create a very fine powder which hangs in the air for quite a time. If you can smell it, you're breathing it. If you're sneezing after a session, it's got up your nose. Even with a mask on, it can infiltrate its way into your system.

As noted earlier, you can help eliminate the dust using extractors, vacuums and fans. I use the 100mm hose of my dust extractor, held in my left hand close to the turning item as I sand it with my right hand. The dust generally plumes straight off into the hose.

Most dusts are just a nuisance and the body can generally cut them off at the pass, just leaving you with a dirty hanky. But some dusts are definitely not healthy. Rimu dust is one example; if you sort the dust issue, it's still worth turning rimu, as it can be a handsome wood, but its arrowhead-shaped particles aren't easy to get out of the system. And there are a few other woods you're best to avoid turning altogether for similar reasons, such as teak (not common in New Zealand for turning) and laburnum which seems to have a bad rep'. I've never turned either.

A good mask is essential to stop dust entering the system, and it's worth getting into the habit of wearing one most or all of the time you're turning. If you're turning you will get dust – heaps of it.

Dust also gets into the eyes which can be irritating and annoying but isn't generally a major issue. Glasses usually don't keep dust out, but they do stop the odd larger fragment of often-hard wood flying up and maybe causing some optical damage.

The other respiratory issue is around chemical fumes from your finishing products. They can have some reasonably unfriendly chemicals in the mix, so ventilate well, use the fan and put lids back on tins when not in use. In time, it's likely the noxious chemicals used in turning will be taken off the market, as environmentally friendlier and health-preferable alternatives are developed.

For ultimate safety where eyes and nose are concerned vis-à-vis dust and fumes, a full helmet with filters and its own aeration system may be the answer.

From a safety perspective, I'd encourage you also to perhaps take a cue from the Pointer Sisters song "Slowhand" (also the nickname for Eric Clapton the great blues guitarist), which, while referring to a more *personal* pursuit, has some advice turners might usefully heed:

I want a man with a slow hand.
I want a lover with an easy touch.
I want somebody who will spend some time,
not come and go in a heated rush.

Not to push this analogy too far, but woodturning isn't a race. If fact, it's a pursuit where slowing down, taking your time and appreciating the beauty of what's going on is a big part of what makes it such a rewarding thing to do. We race against the world's timeclock far too much outside our woodturning shed. It's doubly smart to take a pointer from the Pointers, from a safety point of view, because rushing what you're doing can often lead to minor (or possibly major) accidents, especially where you've got a sharp chisel in your hand and a tempestuous piece of wood whirring in front of you.

CHAPTER SIX: FINDING THE WOOD

You can't turn thin air, so the other essential to a turning adventure is some suitable wood.

The world is full of wood in various states but much of it isn't turnable for a range of reasons:

- it's too soft
- it's rotten
- it's too old, worn, split and fissured
- it's tarnished by some chemical that has penetrated deeply
- it's the wrong dimensions for your proposed item.

An inch-thick plank of wood, whatever the other dimensions, doesn't really have enough "meat" to turn anything but a very thin plate or lots of pens.

Treated timber is not generally advisable to turn; certainly not if the end item will hold food.

You will mainly source your wood from the original source itself – the tree. Not while it's still alive and standing, of course, though you can obtain source wood from branches that have been trimmed from a large tree for example.

Usually, you have to wait till the tree is felled - by man or nature. At that point it's probably an intact trunk of possibly massive dimensions. Lying in a park or a yard or a storage shed.

Someone may have reduced it to smaller, more manageable, but still big, chunks; it may even have been cut into slabs. If it then comes into your hands – thank you whoever got it for you – you still have quite a bit to do to create the final, right-sized blanks that you will fix to your lathe and transform.

There's a point where a log is past turning and closer to rejoining the soil that nurtured it. The circle of life.

Green wood

For a start, fresh from the recently felled or fallen tree, the wood is "green"; it is still wet inside since it hasn't been long since nourishment out of the ground flowed through its woody veins. As we all know, having gone through this with firewood, you have to wait till wood dries out before you can – in that case – burn it effectively.

In our case, green wood is too wet to turn if you want the end-product to be stable. You can turn green wood, and there's a case for doing that which I'll explain shortly. When you do, it turns quite easily with a lot of moisture flicking out and you'll make what appears to be an elegant shape from it. But it won't sand or take a finish in its green state, so you have to leave it to dry out. And then the fun starts.

You see, wood dries at different rates as you go from the surface to the inner part of the wood. Sun and wind draw the moisture out faster from the surface than the heart so the wood fibres dry at different rates – and that's when the dreaded splits, cracks and "shatter" occur. Great rifts appear usually radiating from the very centre point of the tree – the pith – like a starburst. If that happens to any great extent the wood is almost useless for anything but the fireplace.

So how do you avoid that? One trick when you are chainsawing up

the trunk into the raw blanks is to slice out the pith – remove that section containing the very soft central layer from where the cracks radiate.

Left: Pith is not always something to eliminate from your blank; the cracking effecting can be part of the design and end-look of your item. Serious cracks can be filled or glued but sometimes the gap is attractive.

Then, having cut the trunk into manageable bits, you have to prepare them for hibernation and park them to dry slowly. Preparation can include painting the outside of the wood where it has been cut (the bark-covered part is OK) with a wood sealant; this is a white, waxy substance which dries as a clear wax coating that then slows down the release of the moisture in the wood, reducing the risk of a differentiated drying cycle occurring and causing fractures. The wood dries at a more uniform rate.

You have to store is somewhere out of the sun and rain, of course; somewhere watertight but also ventilated to a degree. Some turners (like me) put the green blanks into a bag of dust and wood shavings which help absorb the moisture. Whatever the process you choose, this is when you have to be patient; the wood will take maybe upwards of six months to be dry enough to turn. Hopefully, meantime, you have wood that's ready from an earlier drying session - or you can draw on already-dried blanks from somewhere. How do you know it's ready? There are moisture meters you can use or you can periodically weigh the wood (it should slowly get lighter as the moisture departs) and once it's stabilised, it's probably ready to turn.

You can also get ready-to-turn blanks from other turners who derive a little income from selling some of their surplus blanks, and that can be a very fruitful source of good wood species. Or you may come across some wood a friend has – some large thick planks perhaps or slabs that are already dry, possibly years or decades old. They may look grey but under that outer, dull, dirty surface the wood may well be fine if it hasn't been lying too exposed to the weather.

When word gets around your friends, family, even loose acquaintances, that you're into turning wood (once you've explained it to them – and they've seen what you make), it will surprise you how often they offer you wood. Some of it will be unturnable unfortunately, for the non-turnable wood reasons noted above. But some will be excellent.

Here's a tip too: if someone gives you wood and it turns out (hah) to be turnable...offer to make them something, big or small perhaps. Your call, but when the love comes in, send a bit back.

Here's another phenomenon that might feed into your turning endeavours over time: trees become important to people for various reasons. Maybe they planted them as saplings or seeds and 40 or 50 years later, the acorn has become the oak. Maybe they're leaving their home of many, many years for whatever reason; maybe the tree has died or become diseased or has to go in the name of development and "progress". It's destined for Firewood City perhaps.

Whatever the emotional and sentimental (in its positive sense) backdrop, a tree that means a lot to people may be about to disappear. There's a beautiful opportunity here to rescue some of the wood and turn them something to remember it by. To keep it alive – as I said in the meditation chapter; turners have the ability to prolong the "life" of a tree in a simple and beautiful way.

I've done that a few times: once for a retiring school principal for whom I turned a couple of bowls off a small (surplus) pohutukawa branch from her school. Closer to home (in more senses of the word than one) I salvaged a branch (also pohutukawa) from a tree my father planted at our family home of 50 years at Mount Maunganui, which passed out of family hands a few years ago, and have progressively carved small bowls and orbs to commemorate that place and our time there for immediate family members and their children.

I mentioned earlier there is one circumstance where it is valid to turn green timber and many turners do this. Green wood is *easier* to turn but you can't and shouldn't do much with it in terms of finishing; as it dries, it may warp and crack and end up looking a bit like a potato chip.

But if you turn it to a certain point roughly approximating the eventual shape of the item it's destined to become, leaving a good, solid few centimetres depth in the walls and base, you provide a little room and tolerance for warping as it then does dry out over a much shorter period of time (there's less wood to dry, right?) Come the time to then turn it you have considerably less wood to cut off. Sure it will be a tad wonky, but you've allowed for that and by and large you'll be able to turn away all or most of the imperfections. I increasingly now turn green wood when I get it to reduce the drying time and turning burden later - it's definitely an option.

Anyway, it's safe to bet people will find wood for you – or you'll come across it. But how do you get it to the point where it's able to be mounted on the lathe and the "on" switch flicked?

I've discussed the drying but there's a crucial step in taking the raw trunk, branch, stump or plank to the point where the piece of wood is a single blank that will become a single turned item.

This is where you have to figure out how to cut your coat according to your cloth, to borrow a tailor's metaphor.

Cutting the wood

The crucial factor in making your chainsaw (or handsaw) cuts is to align your cuts with the grain. OK, this is a hugely important principle to teach those friends who might procure you wood (and kindly cut it up for you).

I've had to explain this to friends many times and it's still best accompanied by a sketch – for the purposes of this book hopefully the accompanying photos (next page) will suffice.

Firstly, you need to understand that a tree is composed of fibres – long strands of cells that run lengthwise up the trunk and along the branches and roots. Like muscle fibre. If you cut *across* a trunk or branch and look at the end you see the concentric growth circles but you're also staring at the *ends* of the fibres.

When you turn wood, it is *much* harder (and messier in terms of finish off the chisel) to cut *into* the ends of the fibres, though some turners do because that suits the object they're making. In turning, however, you generally want to be cutting *along* the fibres. That way you're going with the flow, rather than butting up against the ends of the fibres.

But how often do well-meaning friends of turners take a tree and cut it across-ways and bring you some wide but shallow rounds – "already

in a bowl or platter shape, mate!" No can do, buddy...sorry. Those round narrow slabs are fine for Fred Flintstone's car wheels – but usually hopeless to turn.

Instead (*see photos*) the right cut is to chop the trunk into segments that are as long as the trunk (or branch) is *wide*. That will generally give you two large blanks (more if its bigger perhaps), because the next cut is lengthways down that segment through the pith (cutting it out if you can).

The resulting bits look like a paint-tin cut in half from the lid to the base.

Lay each half on its (curved) side and draw a circle on the flat side with a compass – and *that* is your bowl or platter shape.

If you are lucky to get a large slab of some desirable wood, say a metre long by 700mm wide by 100mm deep, like our dressmaker, you work out what the best combination of circles (small, medium and large) is to get the most out of the slab. The same applies to a plank of timber – sketch out the circles that work. Slabs (generally) and planks are aligned the right way grainwise. Here endeth the lesson.

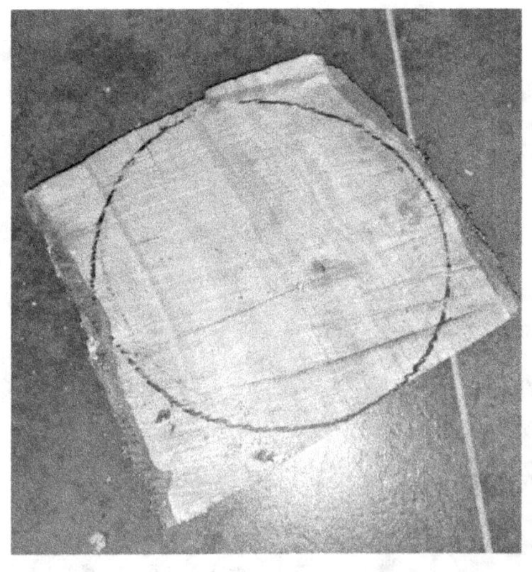

I've talked about tools and the best tools for this job are the chainsaw for the rough cuts and to separate the different circles on the slab, and the bandsaw to cut the blank out along the circled outline.

The early (chainsaw) cutting work can be labour-intensive and messy, as the chainsaw chunders out a steady stream of chips and oily dust. It's also not for the novice, so unless you're reasonably proficient with a chainsaw and *very* safety-conscious, find a friendly bushperson and ask them to cut to your pattern. If you don't have a bandsaw for the tidying-up cuts, a handsaw, fretsaw or sabre saw perhaps can be used with the blank in a vice. If the wood is already dry and I'm going to turn it straight away, I often screw the blank to a faceplate and mount it on the lathe and cut off the corners and other protuberances *in situ* with a saw.

For green wood, once the cutting's done, follow the guidelines above around drying and storing the timber. But if the timber is already dry (from an aged plank for example) you can pretty much now throw it on the lathe.

We'll step through that journey shortly (the core turning experience after all this preparatory stuff), but first I want to take "a walk through the woods": What wood should you be looking for (in a New Zealand context at least)? The news is good: we have some exquisite timbers in this country.

What do you look for in wood to turn? A hunk of raw timber is like a lucky dip: you never know what astonishing patterns may emerge, as in this piece of ash. The variety is literally endless.

CHAPTER SEVEN:
A WALK THROUGH
THE WOODS

Yeah, we have a beautiful country still. Relatively unpopulated outside the main centres. But maps show we've lost a lot – maybe 90% - of the forest that used to grace Aotearoa.

Intensive farming and settlement – the march of progress – removed much of it but we cling to some substantial native forests still.

Back in the pioneering days a lot of the great New Zealand timbers were milled for housing and boats.

The reigning species were kauri and rimu – majestic forest giants whose attractive and workable timbers graced generations of houses (often out of sight behind the wallboards or hessian and wallpaper). Kauri found a place in boats; rimu in furniture.

But, drawing on the exquisite knowledge of the tangata whenua, many other local timbers filled a role in commerce – matai (flooring and joinery) and tawa, totara (carving and fencing), various beeches (mainly in the South Island), kahikatea and a myriad others that had application in building, carving or furniture-making.

English settlers brought in their favourite species so the New Zealand landscape also features some of the great global timbers – oak and ash, larch, fir and elm – and lesser-known but redoubtable timbers like macrocarpa (ex-US), Australian (or Tasmanian) Blackwood and various eucalyptus species.

Commercially, radiata pine (also known as Monterey Pine from its origin in California) was the most significant immigrant, shoring up a local forestry sector and producing zillions of logs that went to pulp and paper mills across the country, or headed for the port at my old home town Mount Maunganui and were routinely shipped to Japan and elsewhere to be processed.

Right: A photo – even a colour photo - doesn't do kauri justice. It is sweet to turn and can have a sweeter-than-honey hue and glow.

But we're here to talk about turning timbers, so on with the show Murray. I'll preface this next discourse by saying it is far from exhaustive. As throughout this book, I'm drawing on my own humble experience as an enthusiastic *amateur* (in the proper sense of the word) turner. I've been turning for more than 20 years but there are many New Zealand woods I haven't experienced, let alone the astonishing panoply of woods that you find globally.

There's also a bit of an upper North Island slant to my experience – I haven't done much with the South Island timbers so can't vouch for their qualities but I'm sure South Island turners have their favourites and can recommend some wonderful wood for turning.

In the bibliography, I list a couple of great books both of which should be available via your local library or National Library inter-loan, or possibly available via Abebooks or similar online secondhand sources. They will expand on this chapter much more authoritatively.

But I have turned more than few timbers, some quite regularly, so here's my ABC of timbers I've experienced. In each case I've tried to provide a gauge of availability, appeal and turnability, finishing properties and pitfalls.

Some timbers I've known

Ash (*Fraxinus excelsior*)

I've turned a little of this, just smaller blanks people have offered. Main tone is lighter – creamy fawn – but it does have interesting – often beautiful (see page 60) – patches of grain. Finishes OK. I quite like it for that quirkiness of grain but I haven't come across much of it. I think it's around and worth including if you can get it.

Australian (or Tasmanian) Blackwood (*Acacia melanoxylon*)

Again not a timber I've turned a lot of but it is reasonably available and the blanks can be reasonably large. I really like it. Great to turn and has nice light/dark grain differentiation. Finishes well with oils or waxes.

Camphorwood (*Cinnamomum camphora*)

Never thought I'd turn this till a chunk turned up in a bunch of wood I bought off a guy in Wellington. Started turning and was wowed by that distinctive camphor smell. Sweet and tending to the cloying but it's tamer now the wood is sealed. Good to turn – a little soft perhaps – and finished OK, but the big impression is around the colours, which are spectacular (in the piece I turned at least) – reds, browns, fawns, chocolates…very pretty. Would love to get more.

Cypress/Lawsoniana (*Chamaecyparis lawsoniana*)

I got a large bunch of big slabs of cypress from a guy in the Hunua Ranges who had felled a row of 15m trees and wish I'd taken the lot. Really nice wood to turn and looks great, with again a quirky, brown grain pattern like arrowheads on the light base tone. Finished well with oils. Probably reasonably available but it's pot luck – not a commercially grown timber.

Elm (*Ulmus procera*)

Another pommie timber that I've occasionally encountered and turned. Has a very distinct grain pattern of regular dark rings against the lighter grain. OK to turn and finish but not super-exciting. Jury still out till I come across more blanks.

Kauri (*Agathis australis*)

OK, now you're talking. Like many turners, I'm a *big* fan of kauri so this'll be a longish entry. Sadly, kauri is a threatened species with a nasty fungal disease killing a lot of trees in the upper North Island. As it is, you come across freshly harvested kauri pretty rarely; it's usually in the form of old boards or slabs people have saved or salvaged from buildings being refurbished or demolished. Swamp kauri is a separate game – people keep digging that up; up to 40,000 years old and while more brittle, that stuff can be astonishing in its colour and figure/depth. Normal kauri is equally beautiful in its colour, depth and grain – amber to gold – and it turns like a dream and finishes well. The only criticism may be that it is somewhat uniform in its grain, not wildly or even subtly variegated in that respect, though I've turned quite a few blanks that have a bit of a blond pigmentation breaking up the amber. I'm tempted to embellish some of the items with a little shell (it often gets inlaid with paua); but generally just allow the amber magnificence – it literally "glows" – to reign.

Macrocarpa (*Cupressus macrocarpa*)

We've just had kauri; now for the poor man's kauri, which is possibly a little unfair on macrocarpa. I've turned a heap of this stuff from timber offcuts (beams) to slabs off felled trees and I like it. It's good to turn and finish (oils, waxes, whatever) and has more grain interest than kauri perhaps, just not that shimmer the forest king has when you apply the oil and lift the veil. That's often offset by the figure you get in macrocarpa though – can be wonderful. Lots around – it's a common tree – and makes for all sorts of applications. Can be quite knotty but that's part of the charm and challenge.

Maire or Black Maire – (*Nestigis Cunninghamii*)

I'd heard a lot about this wood and recently turned my first bit. Wasn't as black as I'd expected but has quite an interesting if not super-distinctive grain. Turned OK and seemed to finish well. I'd be interested in turning more, especially if it does have a bit of dramatic black-fawn differentiation.

Matai (*Podocatus spicatus*)

Another I haven't turned a lot of but have a few platter-sized blanks courtesy the Wellington bundle I bought and have turned one. Turned OK and seemed to finish OK – sanding sealer gave it a nice look and feel. Grain is not spectacular but still pleasing to look at. Mmmmm.

Plum (*Prunus spp*)

Eh? (I hear you say). Plum is on the list? Yes indeed. Like many of the woods from fruit trees, plum can provide spectacular raw material for the turner. Obviously, you don't come across it often, and big chunks are rare, but plum trees do die, get felled by storms or have to make way for progress. I've benefitted from two of

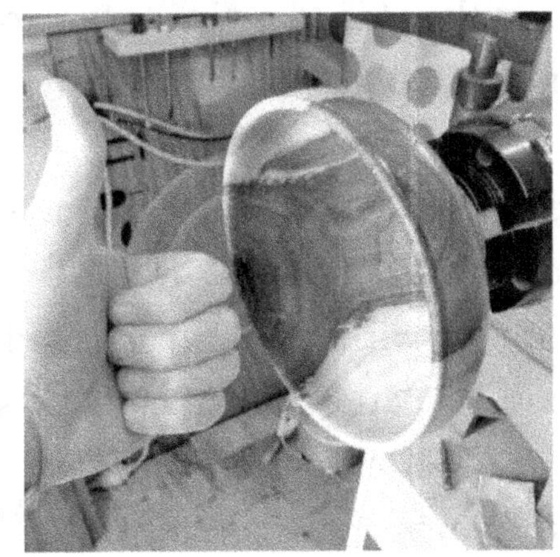

those scenarios. The colours in plum can verge on vivid purple-red (heart) to creamy (outer wood). It seems to turn and finish OK but needs to be dried carefully as it's prone to split and fissure badly. Worth a go.

Pohutukawa (*Metrosideros excelsa*)

The good old NZ Christmas Tree. It was supposed to be hard to get because it's a protected tree and not grown commercially. I've never had any difficulty sourcing it and I've turned a fair bit. Colours tend to the dark red/brown and it's relatively easy to turn though the wood can have a bit of pent-up tension and might fissure a bit if not dried well. Trickier to finish; it doesn't take oils or waxes very well in my experience and I'm still trying to find the ideal combination of finishes.

Puriri (*Vitex lucens*)

Another personal favourite though not everybody's. Puriri is very hard (but that's no issue if your chisels are sharp) and it turns and finishes well in my experience. Like   pecialize, it's the colour that sets it aside: deep khaki green (heart) and lighter fawns and browns (outer wood). It's relatively available, again not commercially, so you rely on friends who might snaff a log for you from the bush or in my case (lucky me) be on the Board of Trustees when the school drops once (for progress...) In that event, I had years of blanks to play with and they were excellent in colour and grain. Interestingly, everyone usually mentions puriri moths in the same breath as the wood itself – seems they (or their caterpillar form) infest the wood leaving large holes but I struck none of that in the blanks I got. Always up for more puriri – it's a great turning wood.

Rewarewa/New Zealand Honeysuckle (*Knightia excelsa*)

Here's another very interesting native that you don't often see but is popular with furniture-makers (and some turners) for its striking uniform patterning of chevrons throughout the grain. Hard to describe. I've turned a bit and quite like it for that unusual grain patterning; it's OK to turn and not too bad to finish though it's quite coarse and doesn't sand up as well as some of the other finer-grained woods. One log I got was a large one that washed up on the beach at The Mount and it had a quite odd buttressing (infolding of the bark) that made for unusual patterns in the finished product. Also worth a go, but don't leave it lying round in nature too long, as borer love it.

Rimu (*Dacrydium cupressinum*)

OK, Mr Rimu. Have turned a bit of this and can't say it's a fave for a couple of reasons: the dust (as mentioned already), and its oiliness which makes it a b*tch to sand. That aside, the timber – as legions of Kiwis will attest – can be quite beautiful both in terms of colour and grain patterns, particularly the heart rimu. Like puriri it's hard and needs sharp tools. It finishes OK – oils work for me. And like kauri it has a brand reputation as a prestige wood, most often seen in furniture (tables, sideboards and the like) – so quite saleable. Very little being harvested so most of the available stuff is likely to be ex-demolition, though the odd log might emerge from the forest after a "storm".

Tawa (*Beilschmiedia tawa*)

Another favourite, mainly for its propensity to developed striking black lines, patterns and streaks to offset its pale colour – a result of early rotting known as "spalting" (*see picture*). "Spalted" and tawa often go together and if you can catch this stuff 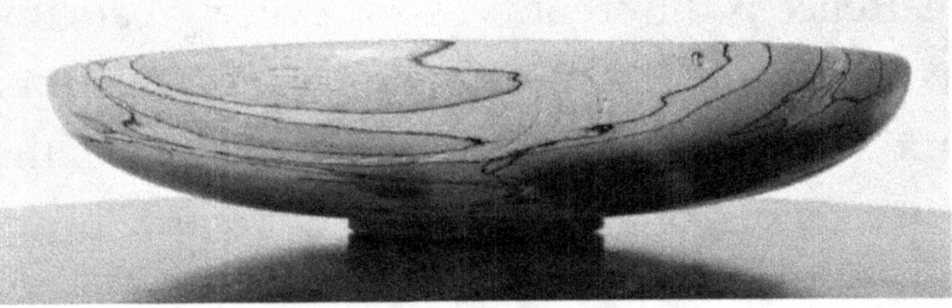 before the rot goes too far (and leads to spongey, soft patches that are difficult to turn and finish) the raw material is exciting. Tawa is hard but turns well and is generally fine to finish, though the look can be a little dull/grey in places. The brilliant patterning makes up for that.

Totara (*Podocarpus totara*)

Totara is a popular carving wood, but I've recently acquired a few

sizeable blanks that I'll be turning. I've made one large basin already –
the biggest thing depth-wise I've turned – and it's interesting timber:
good colour with a lot of reddish grain and seems to sand and finish OK.
Reasonably plentiful.

Walnut/Black Walnut (*Juglans regia/Juglans nigra*)
The last of the woods I can say a reasonable amount about is walnut and
it's a good'un. I've turned both black and not-black walnut and love
them. They look great, especially the black variety, and turn and finish
excellently. Colours and grains are spectacular. I have a large platter
made of black walnut (the big one on page 10) which is wonderful to
look at. My radar is always alert to any mention of a storm-felled walnut.
Welcome it with open arms – it's a princely turning timber.

Sundry others
I've turned a little bit of **Silky Oak** and **Oak, Chestnut, Titoki** – but not
enough to definitively comment. The Silky Oak is pretty – that vase on
the back cover is silky oak – and Oak's patterning is stately and classy.
I've also heard good things about woods like **Olive, Yew** and **Kowhai** –
just haven't come across a piece to turn yet.

But these are only my personal impressions. Every turning
experience is different; and for every great experience I've had with a
species of timber, someone somewhere will probably have had a bad one
– and vice-versa. That is part of the beauty of the journey you're on as a
turner. Lots of the unknown with the prospect of extraordinarily
pleasant surprises.

So, what are you going to turn? Let's look at what the craft will enable
you to create.

CHAPTER EIGHT: THE FRUIT OF THE LATHE

R ight. We've got a lathe, and some wood. What are we going to make? In answer to that, the sky is not exactly the limit, but there's a rich array of turned items that you can turn your hand and attention to.

You'll have noticed that in the book thus far I've principally referred to bowls, platters and such-like – open-ended turning outputs. That's my personal preference. I turn very little on the closed end of the lathe (between centres) but I do make some things in that fashion which I'll describe as well.

A lathe will enable you to turn the following off the open end:

- a bowl which is a reasonably deep receptacle of any size
- a platter which is a shallower receptacle, close to flat – and reasonably broad
- a plate, essentially a small platter
- a cake stand with a pedestal.

Using a combination of the closed end and the open end you can turn:

- a vase, which is like a bowl but taller than it is wide
- a box, which is a vase with a lid (a reasonably advanced project but still do-able once you've learned the basics)
- goblets (wooden wine glasses).

Off the closed end you can turn:
- chair and table legs
- balustrades
- "bottles" (often out of old totara or puriri fenceposts)
- knobs for drawers and doors
- handles for things like your chisels and other tools
- wooden pen barrels (usually on a   pecialized small scale lathe)
- drink coasters
- salt and pepper shakers
- candlesticks
- lampstands
- toys like spinning tops
- spheres (like a bowling ball).

Within each of these categories there is a vast (if not infinite) array of varieties and shapes of the items, and there are probably a host of items I haven't mentioned. Your imagination sets the limits.

It's worth remembering that in its basic function, a lathe spins the wood evenly, so everything you turn will end up uniformly round in its width. But advanced turners have a fascinating range of tricks to be able to turn shapes that are not uniform; that are asymmetrical and quirky. There are lots of books on how to do that – see the bibliography – and online guidance. It's another dimension to the art, and challenging; but it opens up a whole new world of finished items.

I'd like to say a few words on where you get your shapes from.

Clearly there are bowls, platters, vases – all the above, all around us. Mostly pottery or glass but the shapes are replicable in wood in almost all cases.

Once you decide your metier, look out for shapes *you* like and admire – and clip or photo(copy) them. There are no real design copyrights on bowl and other shapes, aside from maybe the likes of the Coke bottle. But once the turning bug has caught on, you'll find yourself taking a much closer interest in circular shapes.

There's a point where taste comes into it. Some shapes can be ugly in some people's eyes. Some lines and curves will not look right; a base may seem too heavy, for example. Working out those arbiters will come with time, but seeing the shapes already made (and approved for marketing by...whoever) will help guide you away from the clumsy or garish. But then again – who cares? The end product is important, but, as this book is trying to pitch it, the *doing* is just as important, if not moreso. Sometimes the end-product is a bit of a let-down. But hey, it's just a piece of wood...and the next one is going to be a cracker!

Right: Just a fraction of the shapes, sizes and types of open-ended turning possible – plus a box (top left).

What you end up turning is primarily down to you. If you're interested in woodworking in general you may see turning as an adjunct skill to creating tables and chairs and other furniture items and don't necessarily want to head down the bowls-and-platters route like I did.

You may like the small-scale world of pens, tops, goblets,

candlesticks and the like, where a smaller lathe is ideal. Or you may fancy going commercial and selling your wares. Good luck with that. In my experience, woodturning is not a route to riches. I used to make and sell a few bowls and platters on the side but it doesn't really stack up as way to keep food on the table and a roof over your head and I'll tell you why (from my experience only, I hasten to add). People aren't really that willing to shell out a lot of money for your average turned item, unless it's spectacularly big and ornate. And there are the "money" (celebrity) woods too – kauri, rimu, walnut and so on – that command a higher price. If you work out your inputs – the wood, the equipment, the sandpaper/oils/waxes, not to mention the labour – and compare that with what you can charge, your labour probably ends up being less than $5 an hour. Living wage is $20-plus. You may be able to work the sums out to make it stack up; I never could. Stay honest and declare it in addition to your existing salary and the taxman takes much of the profit anyway.

Professional turners I understand make a steady living through a variety of money-earning activities associated with the game: they sell turning equipment, tools and supplies, they offer paid tuition, they get a fee for demonstrating or endorsing equipment, they take on commissions (which they can charge a decent price for, based on their standing and reputation), they write books and produce videos – and they sell their turned items. They may enter turning competitions where there is prize-money available.

I decided I wasn't skilled and committed enough to go that pathway – my first craft and profession is writing and communications. And to be honest I don't do it for the money; I'm an amateur – I do it because I love doing it and enjoy the challenge, the constant surprises the wood can spring and the happiness it gives me and those I give my bowls and platters to. I do have another day job I love too that pays the bills.

But let's now get a ticket for an actual turning journey.

CHAPTER NINE: MAKING SOMETHING

The journey from blank to finished

I'm going to elect – for the purposes of this how-to chapter – to describe the journey to making a bowl first. It's what I do time and time again and enjoy doing it. There's a lot of variety in the shapes possible with bowls and the sizes; plus the things they can be used for – big bowls for salads, small ones for trinkets...or just pure ornamentation.

What we'll do in making this bowl isn't far removed in terms of the basics from most other turning projects. But I'll also step you through doing something simple on the closed end of the lathe between the centres – a candlestick.

Setting up

Before you flick the "on" switch, there are a series of things you do to get ready. In no particular order, you must:

- Attach the bowl blank to a face-plate with 4-8 screws and ensure it is tightly held. The centre of the faceplate will be the centre of your bowl, on the top. The faceplate thread goes on the lathe spindle and you begin by turning the bottom of the bowl.

- Set your toolrest in the right position – at approximately the centre of the wood – and lock it tight.
- Get your lighting right so you can clearly see the exposed face of the blank and it isn't in shadow when you are in your turning position.
- Decide if you're going to have a fan blowing the turning debris away from you – and from your face, in particular.
- Put on your safety glasses and don your dust mask.
- Check that the chisels you will use are sharp. For bowls, I may use a roughing-out chisel initially if it's a rough blank, but if it's cut to a circular shape and reasonably tidy I go straight to my biggest bowl gouge. I have finer bowl gouges ready for later when the work is being refined. One medium-sized gauge will still do the job, though.
- Set the lathe speed at a low speed.
- Draw a deep breath.

Now, this book – and this chapter in particular – are no substitute for having a practical lesson in how to turn. It's a skill best imparted in a hands-on way and there are plenty of great turning tutors around, along with clubs to join (see details at the end of this book), to learn from other members by observation on club nights and at industry demonstrations, or detailed videos you can follow. I recommend taking some tutelage in turning at the outset. But hopefully my description of the journey will give you a sense of how it goes. Please don't put this book in a reading stand and use it alone to guide your first turning exercise.

Turning the outside of the bowl

Essentially you are creating the outside curves of the bowl. You generally move the tip of the gouge/chisel from the centre out, though once you get proficient in making the cuts, it's OK to go from the outside to the centre.

Lathe speed should be at the lower speeds to start with – under 300rpm but as the rough bits diminish and the shape is more regular you can up the speed to 570rpm or quicker. The rule of thumb is not to go too high in the rpm if it's a large diameter item; the outside edge goes way quicker than the inside and at high revs can do some serious damage to a finger if it catches you – especially if there's a sharp edge on the wood.

As discussed earlier, the gouge has a bevel which you aim to rest flat on the wood at the cutting point – moving the gouge slightly will engage the cutting edge. You push it across holding the tip (the cutting end) of the gouge in your left hand (if you're right-handed) and the handle in your right hand.

The motion is like sweeping a line of sand on the concrete – steady and fluent. Don't hurry it; let the cutting edge do its work but don't go too fast if it's struggling (if the wood is tough, for example). The beauty

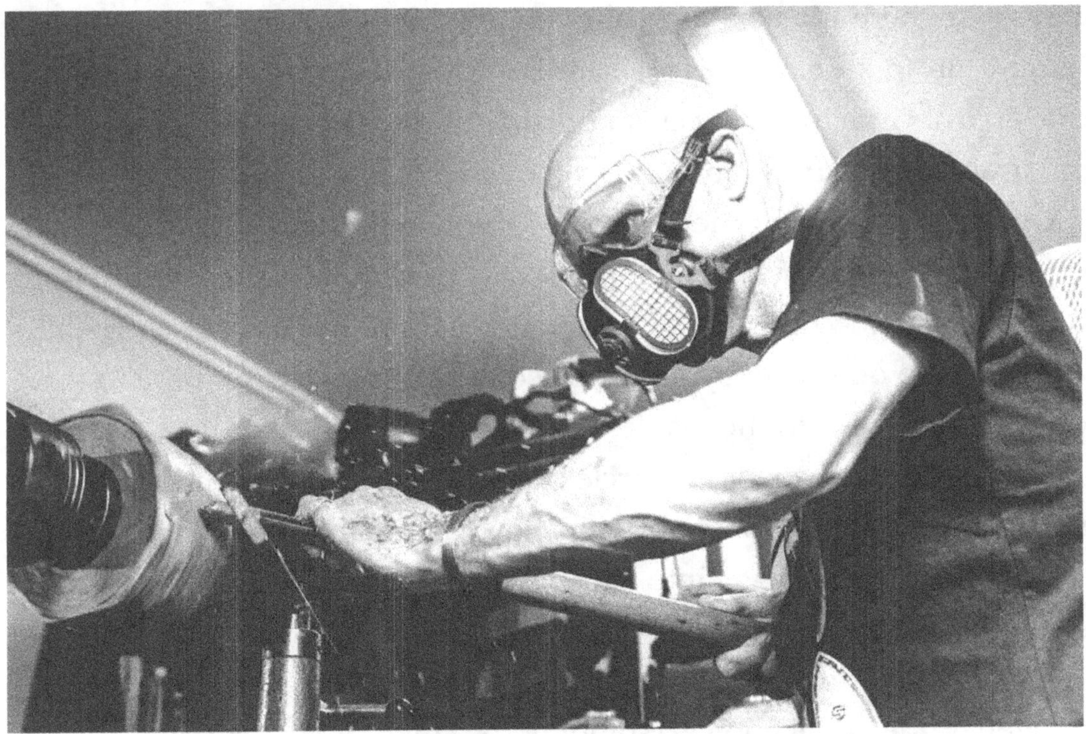

of turning (and it's important from a safety point too) is that there is *no* hurry. Unless you have to turn something by a tight, certain deadline (avoid that if you can), the time you want to take is the time you take. It's not a race or a competition. You *can* stop turning mid-project, go away for a month, then come back and resume the process. The wood won't rot or run away, though (as explained earlier in the section on wood drying) you may get a bit of warping in the interim.

A word here on one of the turner's biggest bugbears: the dig-in. Turning can be like patting a cat, you're going fine, it's purring happily, then you catch on something tender and....*pfffft*! Nice little duelling scar on the wrist. Spinning wood, sharp edge – if the chisel tip goes offline or catches on something and goes unintentionally deeper into the wood, it'll give you a bit (or a heck) of a fright – and probably leave a nasty furrow in your work, which will take some thinking, turning and sanding to put right.

The bowl gouges will get you most of the way in turning the outside, but you may want to use a scraper chisel to take away any fine imperfections. A scraper works a bit like an old cut-throat razor; in the chisel's case there is a very fine burr on the edge that shaves the wood, tidying it up to a degree before sanding. Not all turners like scrapers; there's a pride in achieving a clean finish off your gouges. But I've found them useful with some woods.

You start by turning the bottom of the bowl because an important part of the process is to turn a spigot or a dovetail on the base. That sounds fancy and complicated but you have to create something the chuck can grab onto when you've turned the outside and it's time to flip the bowl over and turn the inside.

That's either a protruding circle of the wood that the chuck fastens around (a spigot – *see photo*), or a shallow circular indent with sloping sides that the chuck jaws go into and expand out onto the sides of the dip (dovetail).

Whether you do a dovetail or you turn a protruding spigot is a matter ultimately of personal choice. Grabbing the spigot is stronger and when you finally finish the piece of work it's a more straightforward job to remove the spigot (I'll explain that later). The dovetail is sometimes a better option if you haven't got a lot of wood in your blank to play with depth-wise. A spigot needs to be reasonably fat, i.e. it should protrude 8-10mm from the bottom of you bowl and the wood in the spigot should have no flaws or cracks in it – if it does, there's a risk it might break off in the turning (with dramatic results).

So you turn that spigot/dovetail and if you're happy you've reached the external lines and the shape you want for the bowl, it's sanding time. It pays to get it to as near to perfect with the chisels as you can, because it's very hard to remove really uneven or heavily scored surfaces on the wood by sanding – it's a lot of work and not always an accurate remedy.

Right: turning the spigot on the base of the bowl.

As mentioned earlier when I talked about sandpaper in the woodturning-explained chapter, you sand by starting with coarse grit papers and progressively move down the range to the finer ones. A sanding block is useful but the approach adopted by many turners is to take the conventional A4-sized sheets of sandpaper you get and cutting them into approximately eight rectangles (about 120mm x 80mm). You fold each one into a third that size, so you have a small piece with sanding edge on either side. And you apply that to the lathe while it's turning. Take it quietly while sanding – watch that you don't get nicked by the possibly sharp edge of the wood, and avoid entanglements of clothing, jewellery or hair locks.

Plumes of dust will come off as you turn and, as advised earlier, try to vacuum that up in some way as it comes off – or hustle it out the door/window via a fan. I hold my big vac close up to the wood as I'm sanding and it slurps up the dust pretty much immediately and totally. Your nose and eyes will thank you for it.

You can also use those other sanding options I mentioned in that earlier chapter. The small sanding attachment for power drills is handy for attacking little rough spots that won't come clean easily; but, again, be cautious in the use of the drill-powered sander – it rips wood away very well and quickly and you can end up with unintended furrows and dips that spoil the even flow and smoothness of the surface.

The small turning device which is similar called a mandrell is indispensable for getting rid of the concentric sanding lines you will get from coarse papers in particular. Many turners use them; the sanding head swivels freely and when engaged with the turning piece of wood will spin furiously itself, and because it's not sanding in a straight line you don't get the scoring – and it will remove any that's already there. Well-known Auckland turner Rene Baxalle makes and markets one I love which has a vacuuming function too. Perfect. More on Rene later.

Once you've sanded the wood to the degree of smoothness you want, you then wipe off any residual surface dust, and you can, at this stage, finish the outside of the bowl. Or you can wait till you've turned and sanded the whole thing before finishing the entire piece.

The reason it's quite good to finish at this halfway mark is that the surface you're finishing is easy to get at fixed on the lathe and setting it spinning as you cut and buff during the finishing process helps get the lustre and finish you want. But there's also the opportunity to finish, spin and buff right at the end. Six the one. You'll work out from your own experiences what works best for you.

Turning the inside

If you have finished the outside, leave it to dry (possibly overnight), then it's on to the next stage of the turning – cutting out the inside of the bowl.

This is where you flip it over and secure with the chuck the spigot or dovetail you turned (on the bottom of the bowl). You first unwind the faceplate from the lathe, unscrew it from the wood and hang it back up, then mount the chuck on the lathe.

You then push the spigot into the jaws of the chuck and tighten them on securely, taking great care to ensure that the chuck contacts the wood at the base of the spigot evenly. This is critical to the next stage because the slightest unevenness in that contact point will translate into irregular movement at the lip of the bowl which, when you start cutting, could give an annoying variance in the thickness of the lip. Small differences can be sanded away but not major ones.

This is one turning trick that it's hard to explain by book, so if, as I suggest, you get some tuition for your turning, raise this issue and seek guidance on how best to get that spigot connection right.

But let's get on with turning the rest of the bowl.

You're now faced with a shapely, stylish outside and a flat surface, like someone filled your bowl with cement. Taking your trusty bowl gouge, you start making the same sweeping cuts you did on the outside, but generally working from the outside in towards the centre.

It's good to do a few cuts first just to "true up" the surface which may be a bit (or a lot) rough. Then you can start removing the guts of the bowl, taking time to trim layer after thin layer away. Again, this is best learnt by doing it under the guidance of an expert.

As you progressively go deeper and deeper and the curlings are piling up on the floor, there's an obvious question: When do you stop cutting and start sanding? That's largely down to you and your design for the ultimate shape and nature of the bowl. You need to leave a certain amount of "meat" in the walls and base of the bowl to give it strength but you don't want it to be too clunky (unless that's in the design). Rule of thumb is for the walls of the bowl to be of relatively uniform thickness – certainly not fatter at the top than further down – and for there to be ample in the base but it also not to be too bottom-heavy. You can keep track of how deep you're going using a simple ruler; measure at the side how deep you want to go roughly, then as the depth increases check by putting the end of the rule against the bottom (inside) and sight how close to your chosen depth you are.

Right: Turning the inside.

A set of callipers is useful to keep track of the thickness of the wall.

As you go deeper, especially if your bowl is going to be quite deep, other chisels come into play to make the job easier (and safer). A ring chisel has a small ring-shaped cutting edge that provides more control of cuts as you get further and deeper into the bowl, and there are more complex hollowing tools which give even more of a degree of control as you are hollowing something out – they are indispensable when it comes to making vases for example, or hollowed items with narrow necks. That's advanced stuff, but if you aspire to turn any deep vessels one day you'll almost certainly have a hollowing tool prominent in your armoury.

The deeper you cut into the bowl, the further the tip of your chisel gets from its fulcrum – the toolrest. That makes the action a little more unstable, so you aim to move the toolrest further into the inside of the bowl to get closing to the cutting surface with just a short length of the chisel past the rest.

Eventually you'll reach your planned depth and through a series of refining cuts will have evened out the inner wall surface ready for sanding. Sanding the inside of a bowl is trickier than the outside which is much easier to get at. The same tools apply as above, however, and after a bit of elbow-grease is expended you'll be ready to finish the inside (and the rest of the bowl if you didn't finish it at the halfway stage).

Finishing

I've talk about the finishes in an earlier chapter, so I won't labour the point here. But finishes are chemical and messy; get your fume mask going and ventilate the joint well. What works well as a finish for what woods is something you'll pick up by experience and from talking to fellow turners.

Some turners adopt a very sophisticated approach to finishing in the way the best furniture-makers do. Many layers of oils, stains, waxes. And the end-product is sumptuous. But most of us, we just want a smooth, pleasant finish. Not too dull but not sunglasses-requiring shiny either. Again, it's personal preference, and experimentation and trial-and-error will define over time your finishing regimes. It's worth keeping a note of what *did* work well (or not) with a particular wood, so you can remember the next time you turn that species.

For a typical bowl, I now either apply 1-2 coats of sanding sealer which I cut back with very fine steel wool, or Danish oil – and maybe wax the item as well. I might do two coats of Danish, letting it dry and buffing it with a cloth after each coat. I've had mixed experiences with waxes, but the right one will impart a semi-gloss and with beeswax will have a fragrance that's part of the experience.

Let's assume you had a go and finished your bowl while it's still held by the chuck. The bits hidden by the jaws of the chuck obviously can't be oiled, so what's next?

At this point, you're nearly there, but depending on what you did by way of the spigot or dovetail, you now have to tidy it up and complete the finishing.

The bit where the spigot is (for a bowl at least) is the bit that sits on the table, so it needs to be uniformly flat and while it's out of view for most of the time, people are going to pick up the bowl and see the underside, so you don't want it to be rough and unfinished. It's also where you can write something to "sign off" your work – the year, the wood, your name, a message to the recipient perhaps. I like writing "May it always be full" (for a bowl anyway).

If you take it out of the chuck jaws there are a variety of ways to clear away the unwanted spigot: you could sand it off (takes *ages*), saw it off, which is do-able but tricky, power-sand it off (also tricky and difficult to get an even, flat surface) or you could do what many turners do now – use a converted hand-grinding tool to grind it away. All of which aren't hugely accurate.

There is another way and it does require a little extra investment, tool-wise: you can get a set of attachments (large plates called Cole jaws with small rubber "grips") for your standard chuck that enable you to grab the whole bowl at the outer rim – see the photo. The bowl is held by eight rubber knobs that can be adjusted to fit the size of the bowl, and can be loosened or tightened onto the bowl in the same way you tighten the chuck jaws onto a spigot.

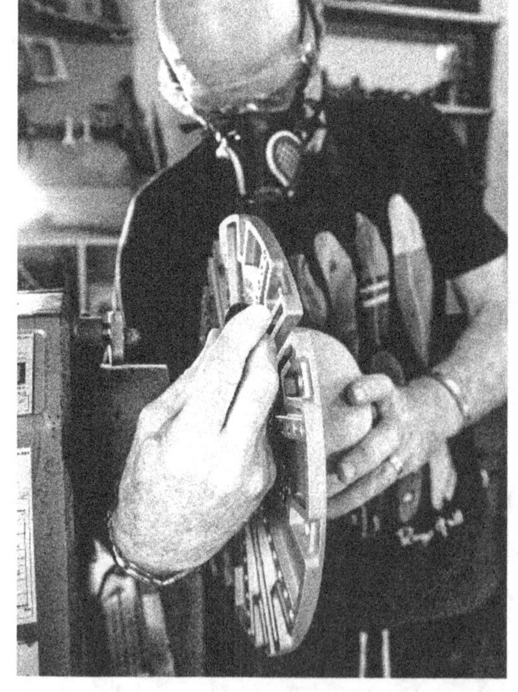

Right: Gripping the almost-finished bowl with Cole jaws.

This grips the bowl exposing the spigot which you can then gently turn away to produce the flat bottom you require – or better still give it a slight concave. All sounds vaguely obscene – knobs, bottoms, expose... but bear with me, it's all kosher.

And so, spigot gone, you oil that last space, sign it off and you're finished. Whew!

Closed-end turning

Let's now look at what happens at the closed end – our candlestick.

For this project, you probably have a long piece of something suitable like a rimu or kauri block, maybe an old banister that's too narrow to make into a decent bowl – or a thin branch. You need to have some idea of the shape of the candlestick; possibly an outline template made of cardboard.

First you have to pin the blank between the two points – the spindle of the lathe at the headstock and at the tailstock end of the lathe bed. For the headstock end you use a small pitchfork-like device called a centre (*pictured next page*), which works similar to those small spiky things you use to hold the ends of a corn cob while you eat it. The non-spiky end jams into the end of the spindle, which is hollow. But first you have to create a flat surface at either end of the piece of wood and locate the centre points. The centre gets hammered into the headstock end spindle, and at the tailstock end you have another centre, called a "live"

centre (because it will rotate with the wood using a bearing mechanism

in the centre) with a sharp point you line up with the midpoint of the wood being turned. The tailstock slides back and forwards and also has an additional mechanism to wind the live centre in tighter. You effectively put the squeeze onto the blank by tightening up the tailstock end.

The centres pin the wood so when the spindle turns so does the wood and you can make your cuts, which you do off the toolrest running alongside the timber.

For spindle turning like this you generally drop the bowl gouges and use a skew chisel, which has a straight-angled blade that you use to pare off the curls, or a spindle gouge (like a bowl gouge but with a shallower flute).

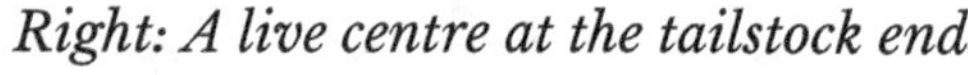

Right: A live centre at the tailstock end.

This sort of turning is different in many ways to the open-ended (bowl) style, so again some tutelage is recommended, especially in the use of the skew which can be a slightly intimidating device till you master the technique (which doesn't take long).

The process of cutting is essentially straightforward – you remove the wood according to the template outline you've gone for.

Then you sand and finish it. Sanding is very straightforward, but remember to hold the sandpaper underneath the blank. The wood is turning toward you and it's tricky sanding on the top as it's pushing the paper at you the whole time.

Removing the work brings into play another specialist chisel – the parting tool. This usually has a diamond-shaped tip which you apply a little like a small scraper to cut a channel through the timber at the part where the item – in this case a candlestick – ends and the unwanted wood, including the bit the centres are jammed into, starts.

Right: Roughed-out and ready to sand.

You don't part entirely through – just leave enough to keep it intact on the lathe, then you can handsaw the last stretch with the lathe stopped and a hand underneath the wood to secure and catch it once you've sawn through.

Where you've parted the candlestick off there'll be a little nipple of wood perhaps which you can sand off.

A much-truncated summary of the actions but that's the gist of the spindle-turning process. For items like boxes, you may turn the main bits, the box and its lid (with spigots), then part them off and finish the turning (e.g. hollowing out the box) using your chuck on the open end.

Left: The finished item with a little shell inset.

That's a basic run-through and again I recommend getting some practical tuition and observing professional turners at work, asking them questions, to really nail down the how-to-do-it. But hopefully this account begins to paint the picture.

Speaking of professional turners, in my next chapter I'd like to introduce three kiwi turners I've got to know and had a bit to do with. To this point I've given you my account of the charm, beauty, allure and attraction of turning for *me*; but there are many hundreds (perhaps thousands) of turners in this country and maybe millions globally, many of whom may get a quite different mix of pleasure out of the craft. The next chapter tells the personal story for those three Kiwis – **Shane Hewitt, Terry Scott** and **Rene Baxalle** – in their own words.

CHAPTER 10: WORDS FROM THE MASTERS

Shane Hewitt

SHANE HEWITT MAY BE THE BEST-KNOWN WOODTURNER IN New Zealand. Hailing from Onerahi, Whangarei where he lives with a superb view of the harbour, Shane has been turning fulltime for nearly five decades. He tours regularly giving demonstrations of woodturning

techniques at clubs and tradeshows. Between demo's, he turns and provides one-on-one tuition out of his workshop, taking time out occasionally to fish the nearby waters – another great love. His business name – Kauri-art – reflects his particular love for New Zealand's most-revered wood.

Shane: I was originally attracted to woodturning by the skill it involved – the hand skill of working on rotating woodwork and applying a variety of different designs and forms to what you turned.

My expectations were that it was a trade like any other, and that you could take it as far as you wanted to. As an apprentice, we did larger runs of repeated work which doesn't suit everyone but definitely builds your tool skills and speed. Turning still meets my expectations.

For me, turning brings a number of positives. I love working from home and I like that I only have to answer to myself. Compared to some trades, you have a smaller workshop space and less equipment – and it's cleaner than most trades like engineering or other mechanical roles. I love the vast variation of turned work that is possible. I enjoy teaching others how to turn and sharing ideas and solutions to turning and the knowledge I have gained over many years with those who are interested – tuition is probably the biggest part of what I do.

There is such a wide range of design ideas that can be created with New Zealand timbers. Reclaiming kauri stumps from the ground is a great challenge. Timber that has been hidden away for many years is exposed for the first time and each one I uncover is individually special. Each block I cut with the chainsaw ready to go onto the lathe holds surprises for me!

It is when the wood is spun in the lathe that the secrets of grain and texture are fully revealed. I enjoy the challenge of getting the maximum out of each piece of timber I work with, coordinating design and finishing techniques.

Turning is my job – my full-time employment, not a hobby – so it's very important to me. But I see also can a lot of benefits and advantages of doing it as a hobby:

- *Anyone can learn how to turn and get good at it; there are woodturning clubs all around New Zealand and a lot of online help to give you ideas.*

- *You can gather your own timber materials and recycle wood.*
- *The equipment available is easy to find and good quality, and the capital outlay is relatively small.*
- *The time you devote to it can be an hour a week or the whole week.*
- *You can look to sell some work at craft fairs to pay for equipment and tools, or you can give items away – share them with others.*

I never tire of turning; there are always new designs and ideas in woodworking that you can bring to your turning. I'm always looking for that in my regular routine and the variety of projects into the future is endless really. It does require self-discipline to keep it fresh – and pushing forward is how I deal with that.

For me, turning is also one of the fastest ways of making an item of value and beauty that I know, but efficiency is the key.

Rene Baxalle

FRENCH-BORN WOODTURNER **RENE BAXALLE** HAS BEEN IN New Zealand for almost 30 years. He lives on Auckland's North Shore and has a day job as a therapy assistant at a rehabilitation centre but devotes much of his spare time to turning, and displays and sells his turned items at a number of galleries. His turning is notable and unique for the integration of woven strands of thin wood or metal into his works.

Rene: *I don't meditate, but for me turning is a relaxing activity because wood is a natural medium – it's nice to work. You may be stressed from what's happened during the day but when you start turning, after an hour I find all the stress is gone.*

One of the things I like about turning is you don't have to measure anything, you're free to create. Making a lidded box on the lathe I might cut a little bit here, a bit there. I like how the shape emerges from the wood.

If I hadn't become a turner, I would have been a potter. But I don't really like the texture of clay. It's very messy. Pottery and woodturning are very similar though; when someone's doing it you can see the shape emerge.

My weaving takes a long time. It is very like meditation; you can't get angry or you would break everything. I have to chill out.

I've only ever had one accident from turning and that was because I was trying to cut corners.

I actually got into turning by accident. My father-in-law had a Beeline lathe; he was restoring a house and bought it to make his own banisters. Once he finished them, he wasn't interested in turning anymore and he had no room for it in his house so gave it to me.

I put the lathe in my workshop and forgot about it. Then, one day, I put a piece of wood on it and started turning. I was instantly hooked. I looked in the Yellow Pages for turners because I wanted to learn the right way and I saw Ian Fish's name. He was a pro' turner – had 200-300 green-turned bowls. I was really impressed. His workshop was great and he had a shop next door. He told me about the North Shore Woodturners Guild, so I joined.

From there I rough-turned a lot of wood to dry and entered competitions to build up my confidence. I started selling in galleries but in 2006 the Asian financial crisis killed everything.

I quickly developed my own thing. I like the weaving. All the little strands are individual but joined together they make one whole. It's like all the experiences in life joined together to make a journey.

When I was 15, I started an apprenticeship as a baker and discovered quickly that I didn't like working night shifts, so I retrained as an electrician.

I currently work at the Wilson Centre in child rehabilitation. We have to adapt a lot of equipment for our clients and I found that very fulfilling and rewarding but it is hard sometimes.

I'm right into windsurfing here at Lake Pupuke on the North Shore. It's like turning – nice to clear your head and when you need to escape.

With me woodturning isn't just about doing it for a short time; when I start a piece I like to finish it. My mood will also influence what I do. If I don't finish a piece and come back to it later in a different mood, the shape will change.

I love turning because it's creative; I can channel my energy into creating something. I like experimenting with different things. Now, I can't just turn a simple bowl. I always challenge myself; it's like an addiction – I want to push to do something different, push what I can do. The end-product is not so important; it's nice... but let's move on.

What I wouldn't want is for my work to start copying someone else. But that's not an issue; there's no limit to what you can do.

I recently got into copper weaving – incorporating woven strips of copper into my works. Weaving is my form of meditation.

What I find with weaving is that you have to be relaxed when you start. You can't force the wood – a piece of veneer like the ones I use in the weaving will only bend so much.

You have to look carefully at the piece of wood before you start turning. Sometimes it's a nice piece but the striking grain or colour might go as you turn; you have to work with the wood to retain a certain bit of grain. Sometimes that special grain only emerges when you sand the item.

Turning certainly helped me personally at times in the past, when I was struggling with depression. I never stopped turning through that time though; it helped my self-esteem.

Terry Scott

TERRY SCOTT IS ANOTHER WELL-KNOWN KIWI TURNER, teacher and entrepreneur who runs his Timberley woodturning business and gallery in the beautiful Hunua Ranges just out of Papakura, South Auckland.

__Terry:__ Is woodturning a big part of my life? You bet. My wife says I eat, sleep and fart woodturning and tells everyone she's a woodturning widow.

I'm lucky that it's my job. Many turners I know only achieve a lifestyle at best; usually their partner works full-time or they have their hands in other pies.

Is it a fulfilling hobby? Yes. I see many a prospective turner come along to our club, little old men who may have just retired. They are dragged along by a mate, they shuffle in the door with a wet handshake and eyes that won't look at you. After a few months they come in with a spring in their step, look me in the eye and ask what I think about what they have made. Woodturning saves lives. The mind gets into gear by the creativity and the learning journey.

I was attracted to turning the way an ant is attracted to sugar. After learning my trade as a joiner and builder, followed by time as a boat-builder, I've always had a love for all things timber. Even at a young age, I could be seen cutting, drilling and making items. We still use a platter I made at age 13 on a lathe I built by mounting a washing machine motor on a sawhorse and using the pulley as a face plate and for chisels some old files I took out of Dad's toolbox.

Even though I turn all the time I'm still passionate about it; like that old adage - "If you enjoy what you do, you will never do a day's work in your life."

When I first started turning, many people gave of their time to help me; now I feel it's my turn to give back. What is not more satisfying than giving advice to a guy who actually taught you the basic skills?

For me, the beauty of woodturning is bringing what is inside a piece of wood back to life. It's mind-food. You can happily do it in solitude if you wish or spread the word, which is what I like to do. The more you put into turning the more you will get out of it.

I'd have to say turning did change my life. When I started, I couldn't talk to a crowd or even hold a conversation because of my shyness. But my work is now recognised worldwide, and I'm being asked to demonstrate for clubs and at symposiums all the time.

Is turning for everyone? Why not? Who wouldn't it suit? I've taught the blind, paraplegics, and even one-armed turners. Put your mind to it and anything is possible.

Pictured: Terry with a piece of burl (or burr) timber from Australia.

CHAPTER 11: THE FUTURE

Woodturning may be an art with its origins in a pre-industrial era when bodgers turned items in the forest using an ingenious foot-pedal-powered contraption to spin the wood and make chair and table legs and the like.

But it's endured, and, like any other undertaking on the planet, keeps in tune with the technological times.

Lathes and all the accompanying equipment have got bigger (or smaller), brighter, better... to paraphrase the laundry powder ad. The most advanced lathes have a knob that you turn to speed the action up or down – no need to lift a lid and change over a pulley on the motor.

Steels have got better, so tools stay sharper.

Finishing products may be heading towards greater respectability in an increasingly environmentally conscious world.

But the Artificial Intelligence (AI) and Robotics world is increasingly taking over activities previously performed by people.

My other great love – surfing – centres on the surfboard; at its simplest expression, that's the only thing you need to do the sport (apart from waves and some shorts to preserve your decency).

But where surfboards used to be hand-crafted – shaped, glassed and finished by board-makers – boards now often get popped out by factories using Computer-Aided Design and Manufacturing (CADCAM) processes.

Shapers may supervise the process and they set up the templates the machines follow. It's a whole lot less messy for them. Hey, that's progress, eh? Nothing wrong with that?

Plenty of board-makers still do it the old ways, but it's hard to compete with the production efficiencies of a Chinese factory that produces thousands of boards a week. So, it's a little sad for us old-timers.

To see the same happen in woodturning would also be a bit of a heart-wrench. But it's entirely possible and I'm willing to bet is almost certainly happening in plenty of places across the globe. Bowls, platters – anything, really, that you can set up a digital model for - could be carved, turned, shaped and finished by a machine – just like surfboards. And popped out in their thousands. Where's the fun in that?

I think and hope there will always be a place for individuals to turn and - as they used to say in handmade surfboard-making - have the odd "sandly in the finish coat", i.e the occasional imperfection. As an aside, if the future is about machines doing more of the work humans do (AI, robotics and the like), a hobby like turning has definite appeal as well – we may have a lot more time on our hands.

Having a machine do the job perfectly to a set template every time would give me no pleasure. But also, machines don't have souls (yet). Making things for others is nice; being paid for them is kind of second prize.

I hope a hardy core of turners keep flying the flag for *handcrafted*, individual, maybe slightly flawed, items. The world's already full of pop-outs.

GLOSSARY

Some common woodturning words and their meanings

- **Bandsaw** – a thin-bladed, electric saw mounted on a platform, useful for cutting out blanks
- **Bead** – a raised, curved band of wood turned as a design element
- **Bed** – the base of the lathe between the **headstock** and **tailstock** (q.v.)
- **Blanks** – the unturned, single pieces of wood ready for turning
- **Bodger** – a turner from ye olde tymes, who used a rudimentary, foot-pedal-driven lathe
- **Boxes** – turned, hollow containers - with lids
- **Burr** (or **burl**) – a large, knobby piece of wood found on some trees, where a fungal infection (like a cancer) has sent the wood cells going crazy, resulting in spectacular grain effects – often like a lot of little eyes
- **Centres** – on the spindle side of the lathe, centres are small attachments used to pin the blank like a pig-on-a-spit ready for turning; a **live centre** is one which turns with the work; a **drive centre** is mounted at the headstock end and is fixed into the spindle with either a screw that goes into the blank or a set of

prongs that dig into it

- **Chuck** – an essential lathe accessory, a blank-gripping device with adjustable jaws (four or three) which screws onto the lathe axle and is adjusted to grab the piece of wood; there are a range of chucks and interchangeable jaws to fit them that serve different purposes

- **Cole jaws** – an attachment for your normal chuck which enables you to grab a bowl or other piece of work (using a set of rubber knobs) and turn off the spigot

- **Dovetail** – a recess in the base of a turned item (e.g. a bowl) used to mount the blank in the chuck – opposite of a **spigot**

- **End-grain** – the grain of a wood seen from the end of the trunk or branch; as opposed to **side-grain** which is seen from the side of the trunk/branch

- **Faceplate** – a round metal plate in various sizes that is used to mount a blank initially on the lathe; it is screwed to the blank and has a thread to attach to the lathe axle; some faceplates can be grabbed by a chuck

- **Fiddleback** – an attractive grain effect named after its occurrence in violin-making (see also **figure** below)

- **Figure** (or **feather**) – this is a grain effect, often lovely, which may be like a feathery pattern or a 3-D effect; a bonus when you strike it as you turn

- **Flute** – the groove in a bowl or spindle gouge

- **Gouge** – a form of chisel; bowl gouges have a deep flute in the tool, while spindle gouges have a shallower flute

- **Green wood** – wood that is newly cut and hasn't yet dried to be finally turnable and finishable (though green wood can be partially turned to speed up the drying process)

- **Grinder** - a bench-mounted device with grinding wheels used in turning to keep chisels sharp; some have a sanding belt as an adjunct, some a buffing belt; indispensable

- **Headstock** – the main part of the lathe housing the motor (as opposed to the **tailstock** – see below)
- **Heartwood** – the wood in the centre of the log (c.f. **sapwood**)
- **Jigs** – devices to help the turner sharpen his/her chisels and do other things to make the turning easier (and safer)
- **Lathe** – the heart of the matter; a device for making people happy
- **Natural-top bowls** – a mode of turning bowls where the rough edge of the wood (with bark, etc intact) is retained and becomes part of the finished product (around the rim)

A gorgeous natural-top bowl made by Rene Baxalle – the wood is Tasmanian Blackwood. (Photo: Rene)

- **Off-centre turning** – a specialised form of turning where weights are used on the blank or faceplate to allow the design to have off-centre (asymmetrical) form qualities
- **Open-ended turning** – turning of objects where they are held by a chuck or faceplate, not pinned between centres (as in **spindle turning**); also called outboard turning
- **Parting-off** – in spindle turning, this is where a **parting tool** (a specialised chisel) is used to sever the finished item from the bits of wood either side that are pinned by the centres and surplus to requirements
- **Pith** – the very centre of a log; can be soft and is often where cracks (shatter) radiate from – good to cut away completely when

you cut your logs up for blanks

- **Ring tool** – a specialised tool used for hollowing-out bowls, etc
- **Sapwood** – the outer layers of the tree, often quite different in colour to the **heartwood**
- **Sanding sealer** – a finishing product that is often used to "tame" wood fibre, preparatory to sanding - but also gives quite an acceptable finish in its own right
- **Scraper** – another chisel, used to refine the turned surface with very fine cuts made by a burr on the chisel's edge
- **Shake** – cracks in your blanks, often like a star ("star shake") radiating from the pith of a log
- **Skew chisel** – a chisel used predominantly for spindle turning
- **Spalting** – an effect found in some woods where initial stages of rot have produced dark lines, streaks and patterns in the wood
- **Spigot** – a turned, circular, raised "platform" in the base of a bowl or platter or similar, used to enable the chuck to grasp the blank
- **Spindle turning** – turning where the item (e.g. a chair leg) is held between two centres at the headstock and tailstock ends
- **Tailstock** – at the other end of the lathe bed, the tailstock is a moveable tower used to secure and tighten into one end of an item being turned between centres
- **Tenon** – like a **spigot**
- **Tool rest** – a moveable metal rest used to anchor the tip of the chisel as you are making cuts

BIBLIOGRAPHY

Wood and woodturning books

There are many, many books on all aspects of woodworking and woodturning, along with websites, videos and a host of other sources of information (some of which in the NZ context are listed in the next section). Here are some of the books I've found inspiring, useful and informative.

Wood and woodworking in general
- **The International Book of Wood**, edited by Martyn Bramwell; (Mitchell Beazley, 1976) *Just a lovely book that tells the story of wood in general, with affection. Includes a section on world timbers.*
- **Wood for Woodturners**, Mark Baker (Guild of Master Craftsman Publications, 2016) ***Woodturning** magazine editor Mark Baker spot-checks the notable global woods turners go for, with an A-list of woods that he devotes a page spread to and a supplementary list of other timbers worth a mention (which includes our own kauri and rimu). Informative and authoritative.*
- **New Zealand Timbers**, NC Clifton; (GP Publications, 1994) *Subtitled* The complete guide to exotic and indigenous woods, *this*

is a very useful resource to understand how the timbers you come across in New Zealand best perform, including how workable and finishable they are and their suitability for turning, along with a lot of scientific information on drying rates and the like.

- **Good Wood - Basic Woodworking**, Albert Jackson and David Day; (Collins, 2001) and **The Practical Woodworker**, Stephen Corbett; (Hermes House, 2002) *A couple of readable and well-illustrated books on some of the broader woodworking skills.*

General books on woodturning

- **Wood Turning**, edited by Pierre Home-Douglas; (Time-Life Books, 1994) *Part of the Time-Life series on The Art of Woodworking, this was (and still is) my turning bible; well-illustrated (great drawings) and simple and straightforward in its explanations (a great strength of* Time *over many years). Spiral-bound too, so great for the workshop. Recommended even 25 years after its publication.*

- **Turning Wood**, Richard Raffan; (Taunton Press, 1985) *Raffan is a prolific writer and videomaker on the turning game. Turning Wood is a very useful companion book to the Time-Life volume, with great illustrations and guidance on the general range of turning activities.*

- **Woodturning in New Zealand**, Brian Massey (GP Publications, 1987) *Subtitled* The complete guide to timbers, materials and processes, *and a companion to the NZ timbers book above, Massey's slim A4 guide is a very handy insight into those three aspects of the game. Some very useful advice in here on how to process your raw logs and turn your chosen timbers, with the author's accounts of how each of the main native and exotic timbers found in New Zealand performs in a turning situation. Recommended for kiwi turners.*

More specialised texts

- **Turning Bowls**, Richard Raffan; (Taunton, 2002) *A more specialised coverage of the bowl-turning game, which is my main line of* *turning. Authoritative and helpful.*

- **Multi-centre Woodturning**, Ray Hopper; (Guild of Master Craftsman Publications, 1992) *The author takes you into a world of turning that allows you to make a range of non-round items, like fruit, oval objects and geometrically decorated bowls and vases. Fascinating.*

- **Creative Woodturning**, Dale Nish; (Van Nostrand Reinhold Australia, 1980) *A little dated now and quite plain but a nonetheless useful guide to embellishing your woodturning bag of tricks, particularly around spindle-turning.*

- **Colouring Techniques for Woodturners**, Jan Sanders; (Guild of Master Craftsman Publications, 1996) *Like Hopper's book above, Sanders takes you into the world of dyes and paints, "liming", airbrushing and stencilling to embellish your turned items. Not a path I go down, preferring (as I've noted) to let the wood "speak for itself", but absolutely a creative option where perhaps the timber is a bit dull or inexpressive!*

- **The Frugal Woodturner**, Dale Conover (Fox Chapel Publishing, 2010) *More of a technical text which focuses on how turners can make or modify a lot of their equipment if the funds to spend on turning are limited. Useful insights and some practical tips and projects to save money.*

- **Band Saw Basics**, Mark and Gene Duginske; (Sterling Publishing, 1990) *I used to have a bandsaw till burglars stole all my powertools shortly after we moved into a new house. I haven't bought one since, but it's on my wishlist. They are a tricky device to use properly and safely, so not a bad idea if you do invest in this sort of kit to find a guide to how to use and maintain them effectively and safely. They save a lot of sawing!*

Meditation books

Most of what I picked up about meditation was in yoga books I read - it's such an essential adjunct to the practice.

There are zillions of yoga and meditation books around that will guide you, but I still think meditation is a relatively simple process – you just have to stick with it and be patient.

Some texts I've found useful:

- **Hurry Up and Meditate**, David Michie (Allen & Unwin, 2008)
- **You Can Master Meditation**, David Fontana (Watkins, 2014)
- **Stress Management Through Yoga and Meditation**, Pandit Shambhu Nath (Sterling Paperbacks, 1992)
- **Yoga and the Quest for the True Self**, Stephen Cope (Bantam Books, 1999) *Actually something of an exposé of the "cult" side of yoga too.*
- **The Book of Yoga**, Christine Brown (Paragon, 2002)
- **The Yoga Handbook**, Sumukhi Finney (Silverdale Books, 2004)

Pluck from these what you will; the value of reading separate accounts about yoga and meditation to me is looking for the themes that recur: why to do it, how to do it (without too much complication) and the benefits.

There are also many meditation videos, courses, classes and online tools to help. I'm a little wary of some courses which purport to teach meditation but have an underpinning religious driver – to recruit you to the faith – with isn't often openly stated. Your call – if you want that religious overlay, well and good, but I personally think the simple meditation arts can be acquired without the need for the additional dogma and ritual.

A final word though on yoga – I'd be remiss if I didn't give it a plug! As we age, our bodies get steadily more cantankerous (do I hear a chorus of assents?!) Turning does have a physical side – not just the toolwork but the lunking of logs and chainsawing, sanding and so on. Yoga is excellent as a way of staying flexible in your joints and strong in your muscles to help your back and legs cope with those long hours standing at the lathe.

EXPLORING FURTHER

In the digital era, the sky's the limit in terms of information on more or less everything. Google and ye shall find...

But it's a wild west in many respects so it's always good to tap into sources you can trust.

Woodturning clubs and associations are a great place to start; they're a conduit to so much that will be of use:

- experienced turners to guide, encourage and advise you
- a source of second-hand equipment - and wood to turn
- a place to socialise on club nights
- a place to see demonstrations of techniques
- a place to be able to learn to turn, and actually have a go on a lathe (clubs usually have several) if you haven't yet got any, or all, of the required gear.

Woodturning and Woodworking Clubs

Most regions of New Zealand have an active woodworking club or guild, and a number are specialised woodturning groups. The following list of clubs in geographical order from Northland to Southland was current at time of writing as far as the author can ascertain; apologies for any errors or omissions.

Details re clubs can also be found in the quarterly magazine *Creative Wood New Zealand* as well as on the National Association of Woodworkers NZ Inc. website - www.naw.org.nz

- Northland Woodturners Club: www.northlandwoodturners.nz; Sec. Simon Peacey
- North Shore Woodturners: www.wood.org.nz; Pepi Waite – secretary (secretary@wood.org.nz, 027 677 0557)
- West Auckland Woodturners: Charlie Wright – secretary (0204 103 5888) westaucklandwoodturnersguild@gmail.com;
- South Auckland Woodturners: www.sawg.org.nz; Bill Alden – secretary (secretary@sawg.org.nz)
- Franklin Woodturners Club: Norm Jenner – president (normandpat@clear.net.nz)
- Hauraki Woodturners Club: Glenn Poultney – secretary (07 549 2048 poultneybrowne@gmail.com), www.haurakiwoodturnersclub.weebly.com;
- Hamilton Woodworkers Club: www.hwoodturners.org; Murray Price (027 488 9432)
- Tauranga Woodcrafters Guild: Mel Yeates (07 573 8188)
- Geyserland Guild of Wordworkers: www.ggw.org.nz; Dave Johnson (secretary@ggw.org.nz)
- Hawke's Bay Woodturning Guild: Annita Frith – secretary (027 664 3375) www.hawkesbaywoodturners.org.nz;
- Kapiti Woodworkers Guild: www.kwwg.org.nz
- Manawatu Woodworkers Guild: www.manawatuwoodworkers.org.nz
- Guild of Woodworkers Wellington: www.gww.org.nz; Mark Wilkins – president (info@gww.org.nz, 021 428 187)
- Christchurch Woodturners Association: Ray Morgan – secretary (secretary.chchwoodturners@gmail.com, 03 366 9795)

- South Otago Woodcraft Club: Bob Draper
  (brightkiwi@xtra.co.nz, 027 418 7502)
- Southland Woodworkers Guild: www.swwg.co.nz; Peter Robbie
  – secretary/treasurer (03 221 7117)

Manufacturers and suppliers

Being at the end of the world, far from the larger centres of engineering excellence, New Zealand relies a lot on imported equipment from the UK, the US, France, Germany and other nations.

But we do have some enterprising, quality businesses in New Zealand that supply equipment, such as **Teknatool, Woodcut Tools** in Napier, Terry Scott's **Timberley** operation in South Auckland, and **Carbatec** and **Jacks** (www.jacks.co.nz) in East Tamaki.

Teknatool (www.teknatool.com) was founded here and now manufactures its impressive range of lathes and chucks and other accessories in China and Canada. I've owned two, and love the current swivel-head model I have; once I win Lotto, I'll get a DVR (direct drive) model. Dreams are free.

Woodcut (www.woodcut-tools.com) make great chisels and are one of the stalwarts of the NZ turning scene.

Timberley (www.timberleywoodturning.co.nz) is an online supplier for all manner of turning stuff, while Carbatec (www.carbatec.co.nz) is a great place to shop for woodworking tools and supplies including turning gear.

The above is by no means an exhaustive list and exploring the various club and other websites related to the craft is well well worth the effort, as secondhand equipment and wood blanks are often available from club members, for example.

Magazines

I like specialist magazines rather than generalist ones which might have a lot of content that doesn't interest me. *Woodturning* magazine (UK) is great and there are some excellent US titles too. New Zealand has a few related magazines: the aforementioned *Creative Wood New Zealand* (a quarterly) and *The Shed* magazine which features woodworking (and turning) from time to time.

But it's a tough gig to run a magazine in the face of the internet's enormous appetite to create websites and throw information at you for nothing and there are plenty of sites on turning to explore – both kiwi and international. Leading turners usually have a site with a gallery of their turned items, tips, Q&A, videos and other resources to draw on. If you're looking for wood, Trade Me's timber section is also worth a look – particularly for slabs.

ABOUT THE AUTHOR

Ron Murray is a communications consultant and writer in his early 60s living in Auckland but splitting his time between that city and the old stomping ground of his youth - the Western Bay of Plenty, specifically Mount Maunganui.

As Ron's account attests, he came to woodturning in the mid-to-late

1990s and has been pottering away at the craft ever since. He's a big fan of the seashore, where he's quite content to spend hours combing for shells, driftwood and other flotsam and jetsam, and enjoying the healing powers of the ocean fringe, the beach and the waves.

Married to wife Jill, a university teacher-training lecturer and administrator, with two adult sons Cam and Duncx, Ron lists his interests outside his work role as reading, writing, surfing, music, yoga, meditation - and woodturning, of course.

Turning Your Life Around is his third book, following the publication of an internal communications handbook, *Talking With Your People*, in early 2018 and a volume of poetry, *Houses of the Small Sea Dead*, released in early 2019. Murex Press is his own publishing company.

Ron's author website *Wryt'ings with Ron Murray* can be found at www.wrytings.com.

ACKNOWLEDGEMENTS

First – **Tane**, god of the forest...nice job, bro.

Then, a big thanks to those turners who have influenced and supported me, and gave me guidance on tools and techniques – **Shane Hewitt, Rene Baxalle, Terry Scott** and **Ian Fish.**

My wood-savvy **friends** and wider family who, knowing I turn, keep an eye out for wood for me and have fed me a regular flow of great wood over the years.

All the other people I've sourced wood and tools off. Thank you.

My family - **Jill, Cam** and **Duncx**, who put up with the disruptions that come with a passionate hobby.

Callum Post who took many of the photos in this book capturing the turning action and the ambience of the "temple" – nice work young man.

And finally, the **bloke** collecting wood on the beach at Omanu in the late 1990s who introduced me to turning – apologies, I don't recall your name. I caught the bug and you're to blame...

MORE FROM MUREX PRESS

Murex Press is my self-publishing venture. Under the Murex banner, I have a varied range of books out, or in preparation. Next cab off the rank after this book will be a further volume of poems, *Piece of Me* (Spring 2020) and a sci-fi novel (*Sleap*) is in the wind for completion late 2020/early 2021, along with a second, updated and expanded edition of my internal comms book.

If you'd like to go onto my mailing list to hear more about these upcoming works and other projects in the wind, email me at hello@wrytings.com – or go to my website www.wrytings.com for updates and occasional blogs.

And, hey, thanks so much for reading my book; I hope it resonated with you – if you'd like to **review** it on Amazon (or on my website) I'd be delighted.

Arohanui.
Ron

INDEX